California
Politics
A Primer

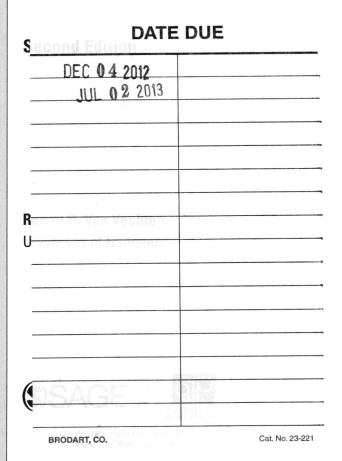

Second Edition

Renee B. Van Vechten
University of Redlands

SAGE | CQ PRESS

Los Angeles | London | New Delhi
Singapore | Washington DC

FOR INFORMATION:

CQ Press
An Imprint of SAGE Publications, Inc.
2455 Teller Road
Thousand Oaks, California 91320
E-mail: order@sagepub.com

SAGE Publications Ltd.
1 Oliver's Yard
55 City Road
London, EC1Y 1SP
United Kingdom

SAGE Publications India Pvt. Ltd.
B 1/1 1 Mohan Cooperative Industrial Area
Mathura Road, New Delhi 110 044
India

SAGE Publications Asia-Pacific Pte. Ltd.
33 Pekin Street #02-01
Far East Square
Singapore 048763

Acquisitions Editor: Charisse Kiino
Development Editor: Nancy Matuszak
Production Editor: Elizabeth Kline
Copy Editor: Shannon Kelly
Typesetter: C&M Digitals (P) Ltd.
Proofreader: Stefanie Storholt
Cover Designer: Gail Buschman
Marketing Manager: Christopher O' Brien

Printed in the United States of America

Library of Congress Cataloging-in-Publication Data

Van Vechten, Renée.

California politics: a primer/Renée B. Van Vechten. — 2nd ed.

p. cm.

Includes bibliographical references and index.

ISBN 978-1-4522-0306-5 (alk. paper)

1. California—Politics and government. I. Title.

JK8716.V36 2011
320.4794—dc23   2011038584

This book is printed on acid-free paper.

11 12 13 14 15 10 9 8 7 6 5 4 3 2 1

Image credits:

Aaron Lambert, CalChamber: 141
AP Images: 18, 42 (Susan Ragan), 45, 51 (Rich Pedroncelli), 56 (Paul Sakuma, John Chiang, Lockyer, Rich Pedroncelli), 58 (Rich Pedroncelli), 62 (Rich Pedroncelli), 69, 77, 85, 99 (Hector Amezcua), 123,128 (Rich Pedroncelli), 135 (Rich Pedroncelli)
Cagle Cartoons (Brian Fairrington): 3
California Board of Equalization: 56
Central Pacific Railroad Photographic History Museum, © 2011, CPRR.org: 10
Corbis: 50 (© Richard Cummins)
Getty: 6, 20, 30, 56, 89,125, 140 (Kevork Djansezian)

International Mapping Associates: inside front cover, 8, 21, 69, 97
Jason Doiy: 71
Office of Betty T. Yee: 56
Renée B. Van Vechten: 2, 88, 94
Riverview Media Photography (Tia Gemmell): 56
Sacramento Bee/ZUMA Press: 52
Senator George Runner (Ret.): 56
Greenberg, Ventura County Star 2008; www.greenberg-art.com: 111
Wikipedia Commons: 56
WILLIS/San Jose Mercury News: 32
WireImage: 56 (Steve Granitz)

Contents

Tables, Figures, Maps, and Boxes

Preface

Since the first edition of this book was printed two short years ago, small "earthquakes" have continued to shake up California politics and rattle the chains of power up and down the state. A new citizens' redistricting commission and primary election system highlight the power of voters and the importance of rules that tend to morph with each election. These changes are fueled by citizens' deep distrust of politicians (generally regarded as members of a corrupt and undeserving criminal class) and are also encouraged by citizens' unbounded confidence in self-government. As this book goes to print, new district maps promise a riotous 2012 election cycle, and moves are afoot to reduce the legislature to a part-time institution, as some are again questioning the prudence of a professionalized legislature. Add in the state's continuing budget woes, and the system seems "broken" and "ungovernable."

Is it? What will it take to recreate a high-functioning governing system for a state that is effectively one of the largest countries in the world? What would it take for Californians to trust in their government or to restore their faith in representative democracy? This short text, *California Politics: A Primer*, attempts to outline the puzzle that is California politics, providing readers with analytical tools to piece together an answer to these overarching questions. By emphasizing how history, political culture, rules, and institutions influence choices that lie at the heart of governing, the text moves beyond mere recitation of facts, pressing the reader to think about how these forces conspire to shape politics today, and how they will determine the state of affairs tomorrow.

Because this book is intended to provide the essentials of California politics, brevity conquers detail. Yet what is included presents an effective snapshot for understanding how the state is governed and how its politics works. Deciding what to exclude posed the greatest writing challenge, but there are plenty of examples here that succinctly illustrate concepts and trends. Instructors may read these as cues for further elaboration in class. Heavy emphasis on visuals in the form of figures, charts, graphs, maps, and photos also allow readers to quickly discern the basics, but readers should also take time to discern the clues to understanding politics and tease out the rich patterns contained in these illustrations.

What's New to the Second Edition

The second edition of *California Politics: A Primer* contains a new chapter on political behavior that examines where Californians get their political information and how they use it to influence state politics and policy. Various forms of participation help channel citizens' demands, and some citizens demand more—and are also more effective in getting what they want—than others. Revisions also include a new section about local direct democracy, an expanded discussion of political constraints on annual budgeting, and a reconsideration of change and continuity that has followed from recent initiatives and the replacement of celebrity governor Arnold Schwarzenegger with "recycled" governor Jerry Brown.

Graphics have been thoroughly updated for this second edition, incorporating major data releases by the U.S. Census Bureau, state agencies, and public affairs research organizations. Some of these graphics, like the cartogram in chapter 7, suggest new ways of perceiving current trends. Many of the updated graphics are incorporated into a new set of PowerPoint lecture slides that are designed to provide instructors with helpful guidance and guideposts for classroom instruction.

The PowerPoint slides expand the instructional package that accompanies this edition. The thoroughly updated test bank of questions contains both conceptual and factual questions that are presented in a variety of formats, including multiple choice, fill in the blank, short answer responses, and longer essays. Adopters should go to http://cqpress.college.com/sites/californiair/ to register and download materials.

Acknowledgments

The clean and vigorous style in which this book is written is meant to engage the reader in an unending discussion of California politics that has plenty of room for more participants. Those who have been essential to enlarging the debate by making this book possible are the expert crew at CQ Press, namely: Charisse Kiino, publisher extraordinaire; Nancy Matuszak, perpetually insightful and efficient development editor for this second edition, able to leap tall requests in a single, graceful bound; the skillful Christopher O'Brien in marketing; Stephen Soucy, a winning representative in the crowded textbook field; gracious copy editor Shannon Kelly, expertly enabled to elicit ever-more elegant expressions; and the production team (including production editor, Elizabeth Kline) who smoothly transformed ideas into alluring pages and graphics. My gratitude and admiration are hardly enough. I also extend sincere thanks to those colleagues who have taken the time to provide essential feedback on the first edition, especially Shaun Bowler, who gave it an important first read, and Mark Petracca, whose inspiration is lasting, as well as reviewers Chris Den Hartog, California Polytechnic Institute-San Luis Obispo; Lisa Henkle, California Baptist University; Diane Schmidt, California State University-Chico; and Michelle Rodriguez, San Diego Mesa College. I also want to thank the many extraordinary public employees of California who helped provide critical source material for the book, from the Legislative Analyst's office to the Secretary of the Senate, to the Rules Committee staff in both chambers, and many in between. Most importantly, I have limitless appreciation for my family: my ever-patient husband, Charlie, who endures my wee hours at the keyboard with untiring support, and Ava and Zachary, who will inherit the political system we are shaping today.

Introduction

Imagine California as one of the ten largest countries in the world. With a gross domestic product of about $1.9 trillion,[1] its economy rivals those of Italy, France, and Brazil. Its landmass includes breathtaking coastal stretches, fertile farmland, deserts, the highest and lowest points in the continental United States, dense urban zones, twenty-one mountain ranges, and ancient redwood forests. Imagine further how almost thirty-eight million ethnically diverse inhabitants govern themselves: they generally distrust representative institutions and assume that bickering politicians will squander taxpayers' money. Many eligible citizens never vote, and 20 percent of registered voters spurn the two major parties by registering as "decline to state." Well-funded citizens, interest groups, and corporations routinely use the initiative process to force policy changes that will affect the entire citizenry. Virtually everyone relies on such public goods as roads, emergency services, and schools, and yet the state cannot pay for all that is demanded of it; it comes up short by billions of dollars, year after year, and voters rebuff tax increases.

Given all of this, California certainly appears "ungovernable." Consider also that a global economy, immigration, climate change, federal mandates, terrorist threats, and a host of other factors place conflicting pressures on those who make policy decisions, even as such essential resources as expertise, time, and money are frequently in short supply. Further, some of the state's rules encourage conflict without compromise. If **politics** is a process through which people with differing

The California coastline: a metaphor for a state that pushes boundaries and seems to teeter "on the edge."

GDP ($US)

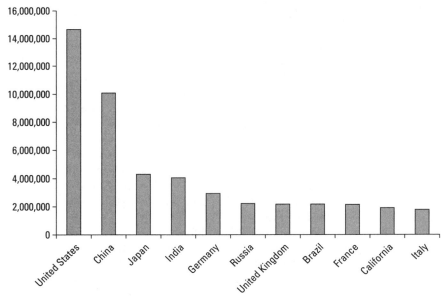

FIGURE 1.1

Gross Domestic Product, 2010 (in millions)

Sources: World Bank 2011; U.S. Department of Commerce, Bureau of Economic Advisors, www.bea.gov/regional/gsp/.

goals and ideals try to manage their conflicts by working together to allocate values for society—which implies that government institutions should enable officials to craft long-term solutions to major problems—then California's system is in need of serious repair.

This wasn't always so: a newly "modernized" constitution implemented in the late 1960s transformed the legislature into a highly paid, well-staffed institution that quickly gained a reputation as a policy and political reform leader among the states. In 1971 the legislature was described as possessing "all the characteristics that a legislature should have," having "proved itself capable of leading the nation in the development of legislation to deal with some of our most critical problems."[2]

It didn't take long for popular perceptions to change, however. In 1978 the people revolted against "spendthrift politicians" by passing Proposition 13, a measure that addressed ballooning property tax rates.[3] In the 1980s, as immigration was blamed for bigger government and rising costs, Californians passed the first of many initiatives that attempted to give "guidance to the legislature" with regards to redefining the state's responsibilities toward immigrants.[4] Legislators were also targeted for acting "arrogant and unresponsive" and for spending money on themselves while neglecting "schools, transportation, and basic needs."[5] By the time term limitations were passed in 1990 (capping the number of terms any state elected official could serve in a lifetime), it seemed the legislature's reputation could sink no lower. Many observers regarded California's legislators as simply incapable of governing.

Today, California's issues exist on a massive scale. For example, more than one of every eight U.S. residents lives in California, and one of every four Californians is foreign born. In early 2011 the estimated budget gap reached the staggering sum of

over $25 billion, representing a huge chunk of the state's approximately $85 billion annual budget that needed to be balanced by universally slashing state services. It is little wonder that in July 2011 only 23 percent of adult Californians approved of the job the legislature was doing, while 42 percent approved of Governor Jerry Brown's performance.[6]

Despite being held in low regard, state legislators work hard year-round to represent hundreds of thousands of people—a job that requires them to balance the needs of their own districts against those of the entire state. That balancing act is but one reason why California politics is complex and often appears irrational, but, like the U.S. government, the system was designed that way, mostly through deliberate choice but also through the unintended consequences of prior decisions. California's crazy quilt of governing institutions reflects repeated attempts to manage the conflict that results from millions of people putting demands on a system that creates both winners and losers—not all of whom give up quietly when they lose. As happens at the federal level, state officials tend to respond to the most persistent, organized, and well-funded members of society; on the other hand, losers in California can reverse their fortunes by skillfully employing the tools of direct democracy to bypass elected officials altogether.

Principles for Understanding California Politics

It may seem counterintuitive given the depth of its problems, but California politics can be explained and understood logically—although the results of the process are just as often frustrating and irresponsible as they are praiseworthy and necessary. In short, the fundamental concepts of choice, political culture, institutions, collective action, rules, and history can be used to understand state politics just as they are used to understand national or even local democratic politics. These concepts are used throughout this book to explain how governing decisions are made on behalf of Californians and to provide a starting point for evaluating how governable California is.

We begin with the premise that **choices** are at the heart of politics. Citizens make explicit political choices when they choose not to participate in an election or when they decide to cast a vote, but they also make implicit political choices when they throw aluminum cans in a recycling bin or send their children to private schools. Legislators make explicit choices every day, such as when they decide to return certain phone calls but not others or voice support for their colleagues in committees.

In large and diverse societies that are crammed with people who are motivated by different goals, interests, and values, a successful political system provides a process for narrowing choices to a manageable number and allows many participants to reconcile their differences as they make choices together. The decisions that emerge from this process express the customs, values, and beliefs about government that a society holds and give that political system a distinct culture—a **political culture** that varies from state to state. One of the features that defines California's political culture is a historical fondness for reform and an aversion to politicians—a theme that will resurface throughout this book.

BOX 1.1 **Comparative FAST FACTS on California**

	California	New York	United States
Capital:	Sacramento	Albany	Washington, D.C.
Statehood:	Sept. 9, 1850 (31st state)	July 26, 1788 (11th state)	Declared independence from Great Britain July 4, 1776
Number of U.S. House members, 2012:*	53	27 (-2 from 2000)	435
Number of counties:	58 (since 1879)	62	50 states
Largest city by population:	Los Angeles, 3,810,129**	New York, 8,175,130	New York
Total population:	37,511,000**	19,378,102***	311,383,964***
Persons with a Bachelor's Degree or higher:	29.9%	32.4%	27.9%
Foreign-born persons:*	27.2%	22.2%	12.9%
Median household income:*	$57,708	$54,148	$50,046
Persons living below poverty level:*	16.3%	16.0%	15.1%

*Based on 2010 census. Source: U.S. Census Bureau, http://2010.census.gov/news/press-kits/apportionment/apport.html.

**California Department of Finance, January 2011 estimates.

***Current U.S. population based on U.S. Census population clock as of May 2011. U.S. Census Bureau, http://2010.census .gov/2010census/data/. Income and origin based on U.S. Census Bureau American Community Survey, 2010 one-year estimates; poverty rates based on Current Population Survey, http://www.census.gov/hhes/www/cpstables/032011/pov/ new46_100125_01.htm, September 2011.

Ethnic Makeup of California:

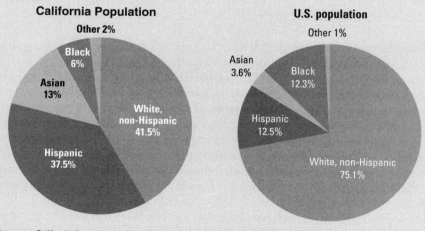

California Population

Other 2%
Black 6%
Asian 13%
White, non-Hispanic 41.5%
Hispanic 37.5%

U.S. population

Other 1%
Asian 3.6%
Black 12.3%
Hispanic 12.5%
White, non-Hispanic 75.1%

Sources: California Department of Finance, www.dof.ca.gov/research/demographic/reports; and U.S. Census Bureau, American FactFinder 2000.

The steps of the state capitol in Sacramento serve as the location where California governors are sworn into office at least every four years and provide a daily stage for public rallies and demonstrations.

Political systems also facilitate compromises, trade-offs, or bargains that lead to acceptable solutions or alternatives. **Institutions** help organize this kind of action. Political institutions are built to manage conflict by defining particular roles and rules for those who participate in them. In short, they bring people together to solve problems on behalf of society. Democratic elections are a good example: there are rules about who can vote or run for office, how the process will be administered, and how disputes resulting from them will be resolved. Through institutions like elections, **collective action** can take place. The same can be said of other institutions—such as traffic courts, legislatures, and political parties—for in each, people work together to solve their problems and allocate goods for a society.

Rules also matter. **Rules** define who has power and how they may legitimately use it, and rules create incentives for action or inaction. For instance, legislators who do not face term limits may extend their political careers by choosing to run for reelection in perpetuity, but term-limited legislators who want to remain in public service have an incentive to run for other offices when opportunities arise. Rules are also the result of choices made throughout **history,** and over time a body of rules will change and grow in response to cultural shifts, natural disasters, scandals, economic trends, and other forces, creating further opportunities and incentives for political action.

Recognizing that both choices and the rules that condition them are made within a given historical context goes a long way toward explaining each state's distinctive political system. A state's political culture also contributes to that distinctiveness. These are the elements that make New York's state government so different from the governments of Nevada or California, and every other state and they should be kept in mind as we consider how California's governing institutions developed. In essence, a unique set of rules, culture, and history are key to understanding California politics and helps explain why elected officials have such a difficult time governing the state.

Is California ungovernable? From online blogs to *New York Times* editorials, the consensus is an unqualified "yes." The current arrangement of political institutions makes it nearly impossible to solve the state's pressing problems or plan for the future. This book explores the reasons for this state of affairs and pushes the reader to ask what it will take to restore government's ability to serve the public's interests effectively, comprehensively, and sensibly.

Notes

1. California's gross domestic product in 2009 was $1.884 trillion. (Source: Bureau of Economic Analysis, U.S. Department of Commerce, www.bea.gov/regional/gsp/action.cfm.) This figure is compared to country GDP data compiled by the World Bank. (Source: "Gross Domestic Product 2009." http://siteresources.worldbank.org/DATASTATISTICS/Resources/GDP.) Comparative rankings for 2010 are also provided by the International Monetary Fund at http://www.imf.org/external/pubs/ft/weo/2011/01/weodata/index.aspx.

2. John Burns, *The Sometime Governments: A Critical Study of the 50 American Legislatures, by the Citizens Conference on State Legislatures* (New York: Bantam Books, 1971), 8.

3. Howard Jarvis and Paul Gann, "Arguments in Favor of Proposition 13" (Sacramento: California Secretary of State, 1978 Primary Election Ballot Pamphlet).

4. S. I. Hayakawa, J. Orozco, and Stanley Diamond, "Arguments in Favor of Proposition 63" (Sacramento: California Secretary of State, 1986 General Election Ballot Pamphlet).

5. Paul Gann, "Argument in Favor of Proposition 24" (Sacramento: California Secretary of State, 1984 General Election Ballot Pamphlet).

6. Mark Baldassare et al, "Californians and the Environment," Public Policy Institute of California, Statewide Survey, July 2011, http://www.ppic.org/content/pubs/survey/S_711MBS.pdf. Survey included 2,504 California adult residents. Interviews took place July 5–19, 2011. Margin of error +/– 3 percent (95 percent confidence level).

Critical Junctures: California's Political History in Brief

Early California

The contours of California's contemporary political landscape began to take shape in 1542, when Spanish explorer Juan Cabrillo claimed the Native American lands now known as San Diego for a distant monarchy, thereby paving the way for European settlements along the West Coast. Aided by Spanish troops, colonization accompanied the founding of Catholic missions throughout Baja (lower) and then Alta (northern) California. These missions, as well as military presidios (army posts), were constructed along what became known as El Camino Real, or the King's Highway, a path that roughly followed a line of major tribal establishments. Over the next two hundred years, native peoples were either subordinated or decimated by foreign diseases, soldiers, and ways of life, and the huge mission complexes and ranches, or rancheros, that replaced these groups and their settlements became the focal points for social activity and economic industry in the region.

The western lands containing California became part of Mexico when that country gained independence from Spain in 1821, and for more than two decades Mexicans governed the region, constructing presidios and installing military leaders to protect the cities taking shape up and down the coast. Following the Mexican-American War of 1848 that ended with the Treaty of Guadalupe Hidalgo, California became the new U.S. frontier astride a new international border.

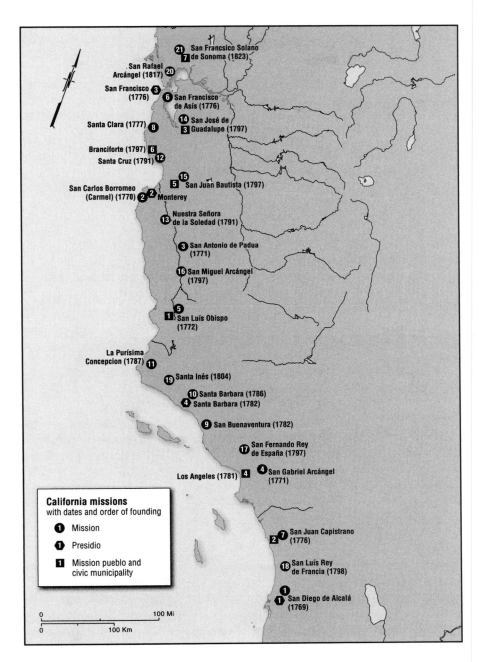

21 San Francsico Solano
7 de Sonoma (1823)

San Rafael
Arcángel (1817) **20**

San Francisco **3**
(1776)

6 San Francisco
de Asís (1776)

14 San José de
3 Guadalupe (1797)

Santa Clara (1777) **8**

Branciforte (1797) **6**
Santa Cruz (1791) **12**

15
5 San Juan Bautista (1797)

San Carlos Borromeo
(Carmel) (1770) **2** **2** Monterey

13 Nuestra Señora
de la Soledad (1791)

3 San Antonio de Padua
(1771)

16 San Miguel Arcángel
(1797)

5
1 San Luís Obispo
(1772)

La Purísima
Concepcion (1787) **11**

19 Santa Inés (1804)

10 Santa Barbara (1786)
4 Santa Barbara (1782)

9 San Buenaventura (1782)

17 San Fernando Rey
de España (1797)

Los Angeles (1781) **4** **4** San Gabriel Arcángel
(1771)

California missions
with dates and order of founding

1 Mission

1 Presidio

1 Mission pueblo and
civic municipality

2 **7** San Juan Capistrano
(1776)

18 San Luís Rey
de Francia (1798)

1
1 San Diego de Alcalá
(1769)

0   100 Mi

0   100 Km

MAP 2.1

California's Missions

The simultaneous discovery of gold near Sacramento provoked an onslaught of settlers in what would be the first of several significant population waves to flood the West Coast during the next 125 years. The rush to the Golden State was on.

The Rise of the Southern Pacific Railroad

Spurning slavery and embracing self-governance, a group of pre–gold rush settlers and mayors convened to write a state constitution in 1849; a year later the U.S. Congress granted the territory statehood, and shortly thereafter Sacramento became the state's permanent capital. Although gold had already lured nearly one hundred thousand adventurers to the state in less than two years, the region remained a mostly untamed and distant outpost, separated from the East Coast by treacherous terrain and thousands of miles of ocean travel. Growing demand for more reliable linkages to the rest of the United States led to the building of the transcontinental railroad in 1869, an undertaking that resulted in the importation of thousands of Chinese laborers and millions of acres of federal land grants to a few railroad companies. Eleven million acres in California were granted to the Southern Pacific Railroad alone.[1]

Enduring persistent racial discrimination, punishing conditions, and a lack of labor and safety protections, Chinese immigrants laid thousands of miles of railroad tracks between the 1880s and 1900s.

THE CURSE OF CALIFORNIA.

The wildly successful enterprise not only opened the West to rapid development but also consolidated railroad power in the Central Pacific Railroad, later renamed the Southern Pacific Railroad. Owned by barons Collis Huntington, Mark Hopkins, Leland Stanford, and Charles Crocker—the "Big Four"—through the early 1900s the Southern Pacific extended its reach to virtually all forms of shipping and transportation. This had direct impacts on all major economic activity within the state, from wheat prices to land values and from bank lending to the availability of lumber. The railroad barons' landholdings enabled them to control the prosperity or demise of entire towns near rail lines throughout the West. Power didn't come cheap, however, and they fostered "friendships" in the White House, Congress, the state court system, and of course throughout local and state governments by finding every influential person's "price." As famously depicted in Edward Keller's illustration "The Curse of California," which appeared in San Francisco's *The Wasp* on August 19, 1882, the "S.P." dominated every major sector of the state's economy—and politics—like a determined octopus.

Progressivism

The Southern Pacific's hold over California government during the late 1800s cannot be underestimated. One historian describes the situation in this way:

> For at least a generation after the new constitution went into effect [in 1879] the great majority of Californians believed that the influence of the railroad extended from the governor's mansion in Sacramento to the lowest ward heeler in San Francisco, and that the machine determined who should sit in city councils and on boards of supervisors; who should be sent to the House of Representatives and to the Senate in Washington; what laws should be enacted by the legislature, and what decisions should be rendered from the bench.[2]

The Southern Pacific's grip over California industry and politics was finally smashed, bit by bit, by muckraking journalists whose stories were pivotal in the passing of new federal regulations aimed at breaking monopolies; by the prosecution of San Francisco's corrupt political boss, Abe Ruef; and by the rise of a national political movement known as "Progressivism" that quickly took root in California. Governor Hiram Johnson (1911–1917) personified the idealistic Progressive spirit through his focus on eliminating every private interest from government and restoring power to the people.

To that end, Governor Johnson spearheaded an ambitious reform agenda that addressed a wide range of social, political, and economic issues that were attracting the attention of Progressives in other U.S. states. Not only was his agenda grounded in a fundamental distrust of political parties, which had been hijacked by the Southern Pacific in California, it was also built on an emerging philosophy that government could be run like a business, with efficiency as a clear objective. Workers' rights, municipal ownership of utility companies, universal education, environmental conservation, morals laws, and the assurance of fair political representation topped the list of items Johnson tackled with the help of the California legislature after he entered office in 1911.

Changes in electoral laws directly targeted the ties political parties had to both the railroads and potential voters. Although secret voting had become state law in 1896, the practice was strengthened and enforced as a means to control elections and ensure fairness. The ability of party bosses to "select and elect" the candidates for political offices was undercut with the establishment of direct primary elections, in which any party member could become a candidate for office and gain the nomination of his fellow party members through a regular party election. The legislature also reclassified local elected offices as "nonpartisan," meaning that the party affiliation of candidates did not appear on the ballot if they were running for municipal offices, such as city councils or local school boards, or as judges. Efficiency, the Progressives believed, demanded that voters and officials be blind to partisanship, because petty divisions wasted valuable time and resources and the important thing was who was the best person for a position, not his political affiliation.

A more ingenious method of controlling parties was accomplished through cross-filing, a new law that allowed any candidate's name to appear on any party's primary election ballot without the candidate's party affiliation being indicated. In effect, Republicans could seek the Democrats' nomination and vice versa, thereby permitting a candidate's nomination by more than one party. This rule, which remained on the books until 1959, initially helped Progressives but later allowed Republicans to dominate state politics despite state party registration that favored the Democrats after 1934.

Civil service exams were also instituted, which changed the hiring of local and state government employees from a system based on patronage (*who* one knew) to one based on merit (*what* one knew about a position and *how well* one knew it). But perhaps the most important political reform instituted by the Progressives was a transformation of the relationship citizens had to California government. This was accomplished first by guaranteeing women the right to vote and then by adopting the tools of direct democracy: the recall, the referendum, and the initiative process (discussed in chapter 3). By vesting the people with the power to make laws directly—even laws that could override those passed by the state legislature and signed into law by the governor—Progressives redistributed political power and essentially redesigned the basic structure of government. No longer was California a representative democracy; its representatives would now compete with the people and special interests for power through the initiative process. The Progressives had triggered the state's first giant political earthquake.

It should be noted that the Progressives' efforts to widen access to political power did not extend to every group in California, and some of the laws they passed were specifically designed to exclude certain people from decision making and restrict their political power. The most egregious examples reflected the white majority's racial hostility toward Chinese-born and other Asian-born residents, which took the form of "Alien Land Laws" that denied land ownership, full property rights, and other civil rights to anyone of Asian descent—laws that would not be removed from the state's books for another half century.

The Power of Organized Interests

Ironically, the Progressives' attacks on political parties and the Southern Pacific created new opportunities for other kinds of special interests to influence state government. Cross-filing produced legislators with minimal party allegiances, and by the 1940s these individuals had come to depend heavily on lobbyists for information and other "diversions" to supplement their meager $3,000 annual salary. The legendary Artie Samish, head of the liquor and racetrack lobbies from the 1920s to the 1950s, personified the power of "The Third House" (organized interests represented in the lobbying corps) in his ability to control election outcomes and tax rates for industries he represented. "I am the governor of the legislature," he brazenly boasted in the 1940s, "To hell with the governor of California."[3] He was convicted and jailed for corruption not long after making this statement, but his personal downfall hardly disturbed the cozy relationships between lobbyists and legislators that continued to flourish—and taint—state politics in California.

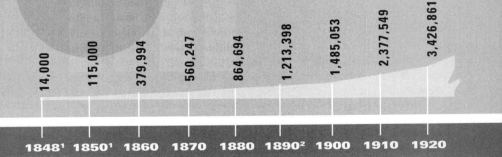

TIMELINE
CALIFORNIA'S POPULATION

1848[1]	1850[1]	1860	1870	1880	1890[2]	1900	1910	1920
14,000	115,000	379,994	560,247	864,694	1,213,398	1,485,053	2,377,549	3,426,861

[1] Source for population estimates 1848–1850: Andrew Rolle, *California: A History* (Wheeling, IL: Harlan Davidson, 2003).
[2] Population estimates from 1848–1880 are for nonnative populations. Native populations were not included in the U.S. census prior to 1890.

Growth and Industrialization in the Golden State

To outsiders the image of California as a land of mythical possibility and wealth persisted even as the Great Depression took hold in the 1930s. As depicted in John Steinbeck's *The Grapes of Wrath*, hundreds of thousands of unskilled American migrants from the mid- and southwestern dust bowl ("Okies" as they were pejoratively called by Californians) flooded the state, provoking a stinging social backlash that lasted at least until war production created new labor demands. The Depression also helped breathe life into what was neither the first nor last unconventional political movement: in 1934 outspoken writer and socialist Upton Sinclair easily won the Democratic nomination for governor by waging an "End Poverty in California" (EPIC) campaign, which promised relief for lower- and middle-class Californians through a radical tax plan. His near-win mobilized conservatives, inspired left-wing Democrats to pursue greater funding of social programs, and propelled the first modern attack ads—the media-driven smear campaign—into being.

Rapid urban and industrial development during the first decades of the twentieth century accompanied

5,677,251 — 1930
6,907,387 — 1940
10,586,223 — 1950
19,971,069 — 1970
23,668,562 — 1980
29,760,021 — 1990
33,871,650 — 2000
37,253,956 — 2010
42,206,473 — 2020

Source for population estimates 1860–2015: U.S. Census Bureau.

Source for population estimate 2020: California Department of Finance, Demographics Unit.

the invention of the automobile and the step-up in oil production preceding World War II. Ribbons of roads and highways rearranged cities, and people kept arriving in California at spectacular rates. Industrialization during World War II restored the state's golden image, bringing defense-related jobs, federal funds, manufacturing, construction, and a prosperity that only accelerated postwar. The building sector boomed while orange trees blossomed. To address labor shortages, a federal "Bracero" program created a new agricultural labor force by facilitating the entry of Mexican laborers into the United States, beckoning millions of men and their families to the country. Their efforts laid the foundations for California's thriving modern agribusiness sector.

Tract-housing developments materialized at an unprecedented rate and so did roads and other critical infrastructure projects. In 1947 the state fanned the spread of "car culture" with an ambitious ten-year highway plan that cost $1 million per working day. Infrastructure spending centered on moving water to the thirsty southern part of the state, building schools, establishing a first-class university system, and keeping freeways flowing—priorities that governors Earl Warren and Edmund "Pat" Brown advanced through the early 1960s.

The Initiative Process Takes Hold

The political landscape was also changing. Cross-filing, which had severely disadvantaged the Democrats for forty years, was effectively eliminated through a 1952 initiative that required candidates' party affiliation to be printed on primary election ballots. With this important change, Democrats finally realized majority status in 1958 with Pat Brown in the governor's office and control of both legislative houses.

Several U.S. Supreme Court cases also necessitated fundamental changes in the way that Californians were represented in both the state and national legislatures. Between 1928 and 1965, the state employed the "Federal Plan," modeling its legislature after the U.S. Congress with an upper house based on geographic areas (counties rather than states) and a lower house based on population. Though many attempts had been made to dismantle the plan because it produced gross overrepresentation of northern and inland rural interests and severe underrepresentation of southern metropolitan residents in the state senate (three-fourths of sitting senators represented low-density rural areas), it remained in place until a federal court struck it down; per the U.S. Supreme Court ruling in *Reynolds v. Sims* (1964), the California system was found to violate the "one person–one vote" principle.[4] After 1965 political influence passed from legislators representing the north to those representing the south and also from rural to urban interests. Moreover, putting legislators in charge of redrawing their own districts reopened the possibility for gerrymanders, the practice of manipulating district boundaries to virtually ensure the reelection of incumbents and the continuation of the majority party in power.

The revival of parties in the legislature during the 1960s was greatly assisted by the Democratic Speaker of the California State Assembly, "Big Daddy" Jesse Unruh.

Well aware of how to control the flow of campaign donations and influence the reelection of loyal partisans, Unruh also helped orchestrate an overhaul of the legislature through Proposition 1A, a measure designed to "Update the State!" via constitutional cleanup in 1966. Prop 1A professionalized the lawmaking body by endowing it with the "three s's": salary, staff, and session length. Lawmakers' pay doubled to $16,000 to reflect their full-time status, and ample staff helped them write and analyze bills. The hope was to create a legislative body that could separate itself from the enticements of lobbyists by giving it the necessary resources to compete on more equal footing with the executive branch, and 73.5 percent of California voters welcomed the political shake-up.

Professionalization helped refresh the legislature's image, but the shine soon faded. It quickly became apparent that these changes still did not adequately equip legislators to deal effectively with all of the major issues facing Californians. And so voters took matters into their own hands, and in 1978 the power of the initiative process was fully realized in Proposition 13. This citizen-generated anti-tax measure forever changed the rules regarding taxation and state budgeting, effectively altering the balance of power in the state by transferring that authority from cities and counties to state government.

Propelled by anger over the legislature's inability to reconcile skyrocketing property taxes and a multibillion-dollar state budget surplus, voters overwhelmingly approved Prop 13's annual property tax limit to 1 percent of a property's assessed value.[5] Moreover, a two-thirds vote of the legislature became required to raise any tax, a rule that empowers a minority determined to forestall any tax increases. This has had significant impact on the legislature's ability to pass balanced budgets on time. Finally, Prop 13 sparked the dramatic use of the initiative process that continues today.

The faith in self-governance and mistrust of politicians that spurred Progressives into action and citizens to approve Prop 13 continued to cause political tremors in California politics. The view that citizens were more trustworthy than their representatives only intensified during the 1980s after three legislators were convicted of bribery, reinforcing the perception that Sacramento was full of corrupt, self-indulgent politicians. Similar political reforms have since targeted *governing institutions* such as the legislature, with the most notable of these being Proposition 140 (discussed in chapter 4), which in 1990 imposed term limits on lawmakers and all elected state constitutional officers.

Parties and elections also have been targets: allowing all persons to vote in any political party's primary election regardless of party membership was attempted in 1996 (Proposition 198's blanket primary was overturned by the U.S. Supreme Court) and recently passed as an "open primary" law in 2010 (Prop 14). *Policymaking* has been altered through changes in the rules. Proposition 98, approved in 1988, significantly constrains the legislature by mandating that grades K–12 and community colleges receive an amount equal to roughly 40 percent of the state's general fund budget each year. And Proposition 39, approved in 2000, affects the voters' ability to approve school bonds by lowering the supermajority requirement to 55 percent (from two-thirds).

The passage of Proposition 13 opened a new chapter in California history by illustrating the power of anti-tax forces. Here the initiative's authors, Paul Gann and Howard Jarvis, celebrate on election night, June 6, 1978. Prop 13's strict limits on property taxes sparked similar "taxpayer revolts" across the United States.

Hyperdiversity in a Modern State

Probably no condition defines politics in California more than its great human diversity, which is as much a source of the state's rich heritage and culture as it is the root of competing and sometimes divisive political pressures. Differences stemming from ethnicity, race, religion, age, sexuality, ideology, socioeconomic class, and geography (to name but a few sources) do not inevitably breed conflict; however, these differences often are the source of intense political conflict in the state. The political realm is where these differences are expressed as divergent goals and ideals in the search for group recognition, power, or public goods, and the vital challenge for California's political representatives and institutions is to aggregate, rather than aggravate, them.

A post–World War II baby boom swelled the state's population even as waves of immigration and migration throughout the mid-to-late twentieth century produced minor political tremors. A marked national population shift from the Rust Belt to the Sun Belt boosted California's economy, as well as its population, over the latter half of the twentieth century. Another wave of people from Southeast Asia arrived during the late 1960s to the mid-1970s, following the Vietnam War, and the most recent influx of immigrants occurred during the 1980s and 1990s, when the state's economic prosperity encouraged large-scale migration from Mexico and other Central and Latin American countries.

Immigration, legal and illegal, as well as natural population growth, has therefore produced a hyperdiverse state in which many groups vie for political legitimacy and attention, for public services and goods, and for power and influence. Same-sex couples demand the right to be wed in the same manner as heterosexual couples; children of immigrants seek to pay for their state college education at resident rates rather than at those for out-of-state applicants; women seek workplace promotions at the same frequency and pay rates as men. In California, those groups that are well endowed with voting strength, money, political power, or some combination of these have had an easier time using the instruments of state power (usually the initiative process) to achieve their goals, which may or may not represent the public interest. Groups that do not possess these assets may try to make a statement in other ways. For example, racial tensions have occasionally erupted into large-scale riots, as happened in southeastern Los Angeles in 1992 (and in 1965 in what came to be known as the Watts Riots).

Continuing racial and ethnic diversification will dominate California society in the coming years, and the resulting social changes will undoubtedly have important political dimensions and ramifications. California is already a state in which whites are a minority; Latinos are projected to become the absolute majority segment of the state's population by 2050. Will members of this group, currently underrepresented among voters, become fully active participants in California politics? If so, how? Will they do so with or without the help of the state? What kinds of political earthquakes, if any, will the shift produce?

Changing demographic patterns have influenced and continue to drive public policy debates. Among the topics frequently and often passionately discussed are whether to make English the state's official language (approved by 73.2 percent of voters in 1986), whether to teach children only in English (passed by 60.9 percent of voters in 1998 as Proposition 227), whether to deny citizenship to children born to undocumented workers (a federal constitutional issue), and whether to allow undocumented immigrants the ability to obtain in-state tuition rates or Cal Grants. The issue of whether or not to grant driver's licenses to undocumented immigrants is another political hot potato for government officials at the state level.

Settlement patterns also raise questions about cultural assimilation versus cultural preservation. Some subpopulations tend to concentrate into geographic areas

A foreign culture transplanted or an American culture transformed? Ethnic subgroups in California have established communities of character, as this barrio in East Los Angeles shows.

identified by a dominant ethnic community, such as "Little Saigons," "China Towns," or barrios. Areas such as these at least partially absorb foreign laborers and refugees, including the approximately fifty thousand Vietnamese who arrived after the Vietnam War or the approximately three million Latinos who joined family members in the United States as part of a 1986 federal amnesty program. Chinatown in San Francisco remains the largest enclave of its kind outside of China. The dual trends of "balkanization" (communities separated by race or ethnicity) and "white flight" (the movement of Caucasians out of urban zones and to the inland counties) have become more pronounced during recent decades and have political implications, particularly for voting (see chapter 9).

The sheer volume of basic and special needs created by this hyperdiversity has tended to outstrip government capacity in the areas of public education, legal and correctional services, environmental protection, public welfare, and health services. Constant and growing population needs will continue to animate budget and policy debates, providing plenty of fissures that will test the foundations of state government.

Recalling a Governor

Prior to the budget crisis of 2009, the most significant political earthquake of the new millennium in California hit in 2003 with the recall of Governor Gray Davis, a dizzying, circus-like event that solidified the state's image as a national outlier. Though the petition drive gained momentum slowly at first, it built on growing discontent over rising electricity costs, a weakening economy, and an overdue budget that contained unpopular fixes such as raising the car tax. Davis's unseemly relationship with public employee unions had also raised more than a few eyebrows, and he had come to be perceived as a "pay-to-play" politician who accepted campaign funds from these unions and rewarded them with larded contracts. Few would have guessed that political mayhem could be whipped up by combining a mild-mannered, uncharismatic governor with a dollop of public disgruntlement and a large infusion of campaign cash, but that is exactly what happened.

Early in 2003 the stalled petition drive took on new life after Republican U.S. representative Darrell Issa donated $1.75 million to the cause, enabling professional signature gatherers to finish what volunteers had started. Eventually, 1.6 million signatures were collected, almost twice the amount needed to call a special election. For the first time in the state's history, Californians would be asked if they wanted to keep their sitting governor in office or replace him; and if enough voters wanted to replace him, they would have the opportunity to choose a successor from among what became an extensive list of candidates. Indeed, much of the excitement came to revolve around the hundreds of citizens who lined up to become candidates, including actor Arnold Schwarzenegger, who surprised Jay Leno and the audience of *The Tonight Show* by announcing his candidacy during an appearance on the show.

On October 7, 2003, 55.4 percent of voters selected "yes" on the recall question, with 48.7 percent of those same voters choosing Schwarzenegger to replace Davis and 31.6 percent placing their support behind his nearest rival, Democratic lieutenant governor Cruz Bustamante. Though the spectacular election season lasted only seventy-six days (a normal cycle is about twice as long), it nonetheless contained elements of a "normal" campaign: approximately $80 million was spent (Schwarzenegger spent $10 million of his own money and accepted almost $12 million in donations), the captivated mainstream media uncovered as much background information on the candidates as was possible in such a short amount of time, and a closely watched formal televised debate featured the top candidates. Yet the recall election also differed significantly from a regular gubernatorial election: low barriers to entry onto the ballot netted 135 qualified candidates, the media focused intently on the process and California's politics, and the electorate became intensely engaged in the process, with 61.2 percent of registered voters eventually casting votes in the election. In demonstrating that they'd had enough "politics as usual," the voters had used the tools of direct democracy to shake up their government once again.

Ready, Set: Action

Arnold Schwarzenegger's approach to governing involved broad, centrist appeals to Californians on common themes such as the environment and reforming government. In true populist fashion, Governor Schwarzenegger called a special election in 2005 and again in 2009 to gather support for budgetary and social policies, though with only one exception the public resoundingly rejected all the initiatives he either proposed or endorsed. The one that passed in 2009 reflected the prevailing antipolitician sentiment, as it prevents legislators from receiving pay raises during a year when there is a budget deficit—a precursor to a similar measure that passed a year later, the latter prohibiting legislators from receiving pay should they fail to pass a budget on time.

Despite Schwarzenegger's inability to rally voters through special elections, regular elections remained at the epicenter of political change through 2010. The presidential election in 2008 drew the highest turnout in almost thirty years, sending strong shocks through the state's political system with the Voters FIRST Act (Proposition 11), an initiative that stripped lawmakers of their responsibility for redrawing state legislative districts and mandated that a new nonpartisan citizens' commission do the job. Voters later added congressional redistricting to the commission's duties. Although characterized by open meetings and virtual transparency, the redistricting process has exposed the virtual impossibility of extracting politics from the mix: new maps to remain in effect for the next decade have prompted a flurry of lawsuits from those who anticipate big losses with the new district boundaries. These protesters include the Republican Party (Democrats are projected to win more seats under the proposed plans), incumbents (suddenly facing a reelection fight with one or even two current colleagues now drawn into the same district), and ethnic groups (African American groups charge that their vote strength will be diluted in certain areas). Courts appear to be the likely final arbiter, as has been the case for decades, and new district boundaries have supercharged the atmosphere heading into the 2012 elections.

Other voter-imposed changes have contributed to the state's long history of rattling relationships between representatives and their constituents, most notably the "Top Two Primary," which cracked open primary elections to all registered voters and permits the top two vote-getters to advance to the general election. Because this creates the possibility that a Democrat will compete against another Democrat (or a Republican against a Republican), and also because independent voters are expected to support less-strident partisans, political observers are betting at least a few more moderates will be elected to a legislature that is at times immobilized by ideological orthodoxy.

Conclusion: Political Earthquakes and Evolving Institutions

Like real seismic events, political earthquakes are difficult to predict. The tensions that produce them are ever present and recognizable in the fault lines that ripple the ground on which government is built. Periodic ruptures release some of that tension. Although political earthquakes may be triggered by conditions or events that are difficult to control—such as weakening global economy, Supreme Court decisions, or wars—the shock waves that these events produce have the potential to effect transformations both large and small.

Political earthquakes throughout California's history have reconfigured relationships between the elected and the governed, between citizens and their governing institutions, and among citizens. Each of these upheavals involved choices about who may use power and how they may do so legitimately. Rules have also mattered: in some cases the shake-ups were about changing the rules themselves, whereas in other cases the rules shaped the alternatives available and determined who could choose among them. Finally, history also plays a role in creating opportunities for action or in creating conditions that shape alternatives. As this historical review demonstrates, California's past pulses in the political institutions, culture, rules, and choices of today.

Notes

1. Andrew Rolle, *California: A History* (Wheeling, IL: Harlan-Davidson, 2003), 174.
2. Quote is attributed to Robert G. Cleland in Evelyn Hazen's *Cross-Filing in Primary Elections* (Berkeley: University of California Bureau of Public Administration, 1951), 9.
3. Arthur Samish and Robert Thomas, *The Secret Boss of California* (New York: Crown Books, 1971), 10.
4. *Silver v. Jordan*, 241 Fed. S. 576 (1965) and *Reynolds v. Sims*, 377 U.S. 533 (1964), following *Baker v. Carr*, 369 U.S. 186 (1962).
5. Proposition 13 limited property tax rates to 1 percent of a property's assessed value in 1975; for properties sold after 1975, the rate would be 1 percent of the property's sale price. These rates would not be allowed to increase more than 2 percent per year.

Direct Democracy

U ntil 1911 California's government reflected the U.S. Founders' belief that elected representatives working in separate departments—namely, the executive and legislative branches—would check each other with overlapping powers, filter the passions of their constituents through a deliberative process, find compromises, and create good public policy. Lawmakers and presidents would compete for power, and these arrangements would safely allow ambition to counteract ambition, as James Madison noted. Spurning this logic, California Progressive reformers at the turn of the twentieth century removed those checks by establishing the initiative, referendum, and recall, thereby creating a hybrid government that is part representative, part direct democracy.[1] What we might call the first branch of California government is the people's power to govern themselves through the instruments of direct democracy. Article II of the state constitution affirms this view: "All political power is inherent in the people… and they have the right to alter or reform it when the public good may require."

The Statewide Initiative Process

At the state level, the *direct initiative* gives Californians the power to propose constitutional amendments and laws that fellow citizens will vote on without the legislature's involvement. Twenty other states also have an initiative process, though each has different requirements for bringing measures to the voters; the indirect method allows legislatures to consider and sometimes amend citizen-initiated measures before they are presented to the public for a vote. The California legislature is barred from making changes of any kind to ballot propositions (see Box 3.1).

Today, Californians use the process more often than residents in any other state: from 1979 to 2010 voters considered 188 initiatives and referendums (or referenda), compared to 148 in Oregon and 96 in Colorado during the same period.[2] Far more measures were attempted but never qualified for the ballot.

Heavier use of initiatives over the past three decades has been marked, and measures cover all manner of subjects at the state level. Issues that surface frequently include taxation, welfare, public morality, immigration, education, criminal justice, and civil rights. Most prevalent are measures that focus on government and the political process—reforms intended to change the rules for political participation or control the behavior of elected officials—and with the exception of Louisiana, it is no coincidence that term limits for statewide officials exist only in states with the initiative process. Taking the redistricting process away from legislators is another example of how Californians have played a vital role in setting the context for political decision making by imposing major institutional changes. Without a doubt, initiatives have fundamentally altered California government and politics (see Table 3.1 and Figure 3.1).

Unfortunately, such piecemeal reforms are forced on government incoherently, resulting in political rules that overlap and encourage stalemate and inflexibility. The bottom line is that the initiative process both directly and indirectly conditions the actions of all California elected officials, who work in fragmented institutions that are not necessarily organized to encourage collective action. As a result, representative and direct democracy coexist uneasily.

Citizens can propose laws at the local, county, and state levels in California. Any registered voter may propose a law (an *initiative statute*) or a change to the state constitution (a *constitutional amendment*). However, because most citizens cannot overcome the financial and time barriers associated with the initiative process, well-funded interest groups now dominate a system that was intended to *reduce* their influence. Special interest groups, corporations, wealthy individuals, political parties, and even elected officials use the state's initiative process to circumvent regular lawmaking channels because it "is the only way for [them] to get the policy they want."[3] Though the process remains primarily a check against government corruption and unresponsiveness, the Progressives of the late nineteenth and early twentieth centuries would probably be surprised at how the process works today.

Preparation Stage

The first step in bringing an idea to the ballot is drafting, or writing, the text of the proposed law. Measures are worded carefully to fit the needs and goals

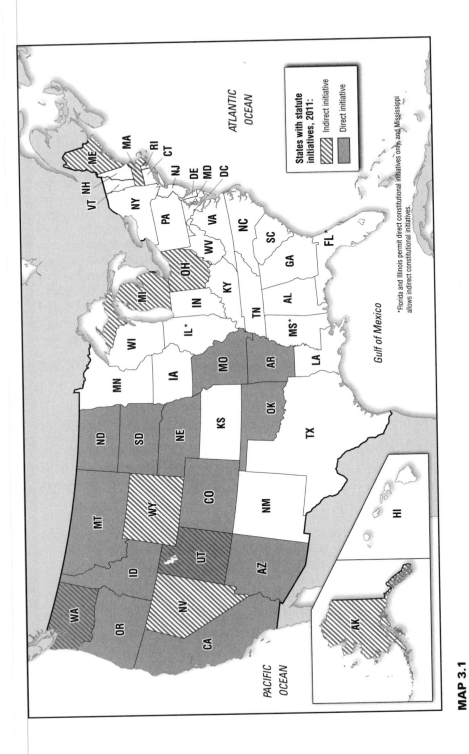

MAP 3.1

States with the Initiative Process, 2011

States with statute initiatives, 2011:
- Indirect initiative
- Direct initiative

*Florida and Illinois permit direct constitutional initiatives only, and Mississippi allows indirect constitutional initiatives.

PACIFIC OCEAN

ATLANTIC OCEAN

Gulf of Mexico

TABLE 3.1 Selected Landmark Initiatives in California, 1966–2010

Number	Description	Year
Proposition 1A	Constitutional reform, legislative professionalization	1966
Prop 9	Political reform act	1974
Prop 13	Property tax limitation	1978
Prop 98	Minimum annual funding levels for education	1988
Prop 140	State officeholder term limits	1990
Prop 184	Three strikes law	1994
Prop 187	Ineligibility of illegal aliens for public services	1994
Prop 209	Ending affirmative action in state institutions	1996
Prop 215	Medical use of marijuana	1996
Prop 5	Tribal state gaming compacts, tribal casinos	1998
Prop 227	Elimination of bilingual education	1998
Props 11, 20	Citizens' redistricting commission (state and congressional districts)	2008, 2010
Prop 8	Definition of marriage	2009
Prop 14	Open primary elections	2010

of their sponsors, and it is the authors' responsibility to correct errors or ambiguities that may later provide opponents with a convenient excuse to challenge them in court. A proposed initiative must be submitted with $200 to the attorney general's office, where it is assigned a title and summary that captures the measure's purpose, and from that point on the wording of a proposed law cannot be changed. The state also prepares a fiscal analysis of the proposed law if the attorney general requests one.

Qualification Stage

During the qualification stage, the initiative's proponents must circulate strictly formatted petitions throughout the state and gather enough valid voter signatures to qualify the measure for the ballot. Signature requirements are based on a percentage of all votes cast for governor during the previous election: the requirement is 5 percent (504,760 signatures, based on the 2010 gubernatorial election) for an initiative

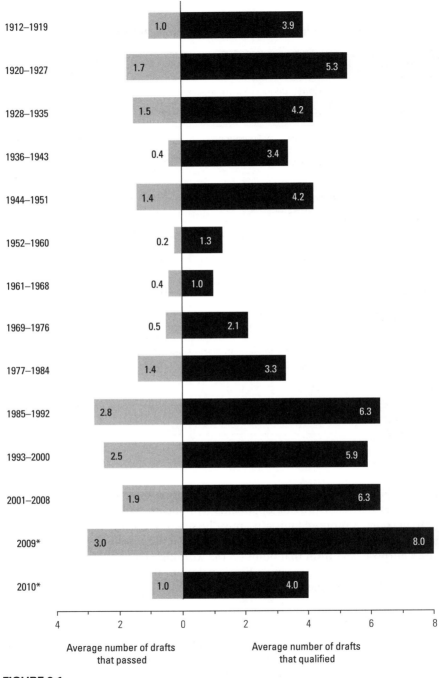

FIGURE 3.1
Initiatives Approved, 1912–2010

Source: California Secretary of State.

* Actual numbers rather than the average number are reported for 2009 and 2010.

OFFICIAL BALLOT

SAN DIEGO COUNTY, CALIFORNIA
PRESIDENTIAL GENERAL ELECTION - November 4, 2008

MEASURES SUBMITTED TO THE VOTERS

STATE

STATE

PROP 8 ELIMINATES RIGHT OF SAME-SEX COUPLES TO MARRY. INITIATIVE CONSTITUTIONAL AMENDMENT. Changes California Constitution to eliminate the right of same-sex couples to marry. Provides that only marriage between a man and a women is valid or recognized in California. Fiscal Impact: Over next few years, potential revenue loss, mainly sales taxes, totaling in the several tens of millions of dollars, to state and local goverments. In the long run, likely little fiscal impact on state and local governments.

YES ⬭

NO ⬭

PROP 9 CRIMINAL JUSTICE SYSTEM. VICTIMS' RIGHTS. PAROLE INITIATIVE CONSTITUTIONAL AMENDMENT AND STATUTE. Requires notification to victim and opportunity for input during phases of criminal justice process,including bail, pleas, sentencing and parole. Establishes victim safety as consideration for bail or parole. Fiscal Impact: Potential loss of state savings on prison operations and increased county jail costs amounting to hundreds of millions of dollars annually. Potential net savings in the low tens of millions of dollars annually on parole procedures.

YES ⬭

NO ⬭

PROP 10 ALTERNATIVE FUEL VEHICLES AND RENEWABLE ENERGY BONDS. INITIATIVE STATUTE. Authorizes $5 billion in bonds paid from state's General Fund, to help consumers and others purchase certain vehicles, and to fund research in renewable energy and alternative fuel vehicles. Fiscal Impact: State cost of about $10 billion over 30 years to repay bonds. Increased state and local revenues, potentially totaling several tens of millions of dollars through 2019. Potential state administrative costs up to about $10 million annually.

YES ⬭

NO ⬭

PROP 11 REDISTRICTING. INITIATIVE CONSTITUTIONAL AMENDMENT AND STATUTE. Changes authority for establishing state office boundaries from elected representatives to commission. Establishes multilevel process to select commissioners from registered voter pool. Commission comprised of Democrats, Republicans, and representatives of neither party. Fiscal Impact: Potential increase in state redistricting costs once every ten years due to two entities performing redistricting. Any increase in costs probably would not be significant.

YES ⬭

NO ⬭

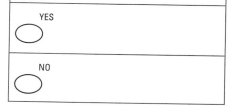

FIGURE 3.2
Sample Ballot with Initiatives

Emotions ran high on both sides as the vote on Proposition 8, a measure banning same-sex marriage, neared. Voters narrowly approved it in November 2008, 52.3 percent to 47.7 percent. Supporters of same-sex marriage vowed to "bring it back to the ballot" again.

and 8 percent (807,615 signatures) for a constitutional amendment. Proponents have 150 days to circulate and collect signatures on their formal petitions. To complicate matters a bit, each person who signs a petition must be a registered voter in the county where the petition is signed, and completed petitions must be submitted to the appropriate elections official (typically the county clerk or registrar of voters) in the county where each petition was filled out. The secretary of state must receive and verify the signatures at least 131 days before the next general or special election. Proponents usually hire signature-gathering firms to help with the legwork, and the rule of thumb is to gather twice as many signatures as required because many will be invalidated later. At an average cost of $1 to $2 per signature, it can easily cost $2 million or more to qualify a measure. If the secretary of state determines that enough registered voters signed the filed petitions, the measure is certified, given a number, and becomes known as "Proposition [number]." As of 2012, initiatives will no longer appear on primary election ballots.

Campaigning Stage

Most initiative attempts fail during the qualification stage, but for successful proponents, the campaigning stage begins the moment the secretary of state certifies their measure, and in the coming months they will usually raise and spend millions of dollars to mobilize or sway voters. A thriving initiative industry has grown around the need to coordinate fund-raising, television and radio advertising, and mass mailings. The cost of initiative campaigns has skyrocketed in recent decades, and the most expensive in U.S. history have taken place in California (see Table 3.2). It is not uncommon for supporters and opponents to spend between $50 million and $100 million combined on highly controversial measures; in 2008 approximately $83 million was spent on Proposition 8, a constitutional amendment banning same-sex marriage. Not surprisingly, more money tends to be spent when industries are directly affected in some way, whereas uncontroversial measures tend to attract little or no spending.

The Power of the Initiative Process

Only a simple majority is needed to pass an initiative or a recall, but supermajorities (two-thirds vote) are required for general obligation bonds and most school bonds (55 percent). Initiative laws generally take effect the day after they are approved, unlike bills, which normally go into effect on January 1 the following year. Election results don't always settle issues, however. Opponents often file lawsuits as soon as the votes are counted, triggering expensive court battles over a measure's constitutionality, meaning, or validity. These battles can last years and may result in partial or total invalidation of the measure. Public officials may also search for ways to get around laws they find objectionable, and there is always the likelihood that a contentious issue will be revisited in a future proposition because new laws often have

TABLE 3.2 Five Most Expensive Ballot Measure Campaigns*

Proposition	Election year	Subject	Total spent	Proponents	Opponents	Pass/ fail (% margin)
87	2006	Alternative energy	$154,199,199	$61,251,188	$92,948,011	F (45/55)
5	1998	Indian gaming	$114,012,698	$81,316,570	$32,696,128	P (62/38)
8	2008	Same-sex marriage ban	$77,566,120	$36,285,220	$41,280,900	P (52/48)
86	2006	Tobacco tax	$82,748,301	$16,446,205	$66,302,096	F (48/52)
38	2000	School vouchers	$76,428,996	$37,489,136	$38,939,860	F (29/71)

Source: Proposition 8 figures from the *Los Angeles Times*, http://theenvelope.latimes.com/la-moneymap,0,4156785. htmlstory, adjusted to 2006 dollars. All other figures from *Democracy by Initiative: Shaping California's Fourth Branch of Government*, 2nd ed. (Los Angeles: Center for Governmental Studies, 2008). Available online at www.cgs.org/images/publications/cgs_dbi_full_book_f.pdf.

*All figures have been adjusted to 2006 dollars.

unintended consequences and because losers always have another chance to prevail.

Initiative use is robust for other reasons. Aspiring politicians and lawmakers build their reputations by sponsoring propositions that can't get traction in the legislature. Corporations and special interest groups find them appealing because they know that successful measures can translate into financial gain or more friendly regulation. Competition also plays a role: at times adversaries take their fights to the ballot with dueling measures that propose very different solutions to a problem, as seen in the rival discount prescription drug measures proposed in 2006—one backed by consumer groups, the other by pharmaceutical companies (Props 75 and 79). Only rarely do grassroots movements mushroom into initiative movements, and even those tend to be elite- or activist-driven efforts. Still, such movements can have enormous consequences for governing.

Today, the power of the average voter has been eclipsed by industry initiative activity and special interest group imperatives. Voters endure campaigns waged by corporations with deep pockets and media barrages containing oversimplified messages. Armed only with these biased accounts, they must decide on complex policies frequently crafted without the benefit of compromise, and these policies may set rules that are difficult to amend later. Not surprisingly, confused voters tend to vote "no," especially when the ramifications of voting "yes" are not clear. Most citizens believe there are too many propositions, that the ballot wording is too complicated, and that the initiative process is in need of either minor or major changes.[4]

Given California's history, it is only a matter of time before citizens further reform the process (see Box 3.1). In 2012 the process will reflect one major change: initiatives will not be allowed to appear on primary election ballots. They will appear in general elections or in special elections called by the governor.

Referendum

Citizens may also reject or approve laws or parts of laws. To prompt a referendum, petitioners must collect the same number of signatures required for initiatives (504,760) within three months. If it qualifies for the ballot, voters will decide whether a particular legislative act should be rejected. **Petition referenda** are rare: only forty-seven measures have qualified for the ballot since 1912, and voters have historically been more likely to repeal a law than approve it (59.6 percent of laws were rejected through referenda; 40.4 percent were approved). Far more common are **bond measures** that are first approved by the legislature and then passed along to voters for approval. The constitution requires that voters approve state borrowing above $300,000. Bond measures authorize the state treasurer to sell bonds on the open market, which essentially are promises to pay back with interest any amounts loaned to the state. Bonds are typically used to finance multimillion- or billion-dollar infrastructure projects ranging from water restoration to library renovation, and since 2000 the average bond has cost more than $5 billion (see chapter 8). During recent budget crises the state borrowed billions through the sale of bonds in order to close budget gaps. Most bond measures generate little controversy and around 60 percent pass. However, financing state government projects with billion-dollar bonds contains substantial penalties: taxpayers will end up paying twice the face amount of what is borrowed after the interest and capital are repaid, and a growing, sizable share of the state's annual budget each year is dedicated to paying off interest, or "servicing the debt."

Recall

California is one of nineteen states allowing voters to remove and replace state elected officials between regular elections, and it is one of at least twenty-nine permitting the recall of local officials.[5] In a California recall election, voters are asked whether the official in question should be removed from office; they may then choose a replacement from an official list of candidates, regardless of whether they cast an initial "yes" or "no" vote. Nationwide, the majority of recall attempts are aimed at local officials such as justices, city council members, or school board members; state officials are also frequently targeted, albeit unsuccessfully.

Low recall success rates are partly ensured through fairly high signature requirements and relatively short deadlines. For lawmakers and appeals court judges in California for instance, petitioners have 160 days to meet the signature threshold,

```
                            SAMPLE

        STATEWIDE SPECIAL ELECTION - OCTOBER 7, 2003 - SAN DIEGO COUNTY
                            OFFICIAL BALLOT

                              STATE

        VOTE YES OR NO ON THE RECALL MEASURE BELOW
        ┌─────────────────────────────────────────┬───┬───────────┐
        │ Shall  GRAY  DAVIS  be  recalled (removed)│ 3 │ YES ➡ ○  │
        │ from the office of Governor?              ├───┼───────────┤
        │                                           │ 4 │ NO ➡ ○   │
        └─────────────────────────────────────────┴───┴───────────┘

            THE CANDIDATES TO SUCCEED (REPLACE) GRAY DAVIS
         IF HE IS RECALLED (REMOVED) ARE LISTED ON THIS PAGE
                    AND THE FOLLOWING 6 PAGES
```

FIGURE 3.3

2003 Governor Recall Measure Question on the Sample Ballot

which is equal to 20 percent of the votes cast in the last election for the official being recalled. For statewide officials, signatures must be obtained from voters in at least five different counties, with minimums in each jurisdiction tied to the prior election results. The requirements tend to be higher for recalling governors; in some states the signature threshold to bring about a recall is as high as 40 percent of eligible voters. Citizens wishing to recall a governor in California have a little more than five months to submit valid signatures equal to 12 percent of the votes cast during the previous gubernatorial election (more than 1.2 million signatures based on the 2010 election).

No specific grounds for removal are needed to launch a recall in California, but proponents must state their reasons on the petitions they circulate. Since 1913, 154 recalls have been launched against state elected officials in California, but only nine of these qualified for the ballot and only five ultimately succeeded. The most recent target was Republican state senator Jeffrey Dunham, who survived a recall election in 2008, but by far the most dramatic was the 2003 recall of Governor Gray Davis, discussed earlier in chapter 2. Ironically, it takes a majority vote to remove an incumbent, but the replacement wins by plurality vote (the most votes of all cast), so Arnold Schwarzenegger could have won with far less than the 48.7 percent he received in an election that featured 135 candidates.

Direct Democracy at the Local Level

Direct democracy also exists in all California counties and municipalities, though its use seldom sparks intense interest. Controversial decisions on school boards lead

BOX 3.1 Reforming the Initiative Process

Is the initiative process ripe for reform? Californians overwhelmingly support their right to make laws alongside the state legislature, but many acknowledge the process isn't perfect. Its built-in biases have long been recognized, and resource-rich special interests have advantages over average citizens at every stage, a situation that contradicts the original intent of empowering the many at the expense of the few. Fixing these problems and others will require balancing individual power and free-speech rights. Opinion is sharply divided over whether and how to address these complex issues and how effective any solutions would be.

Problems and Suggested Remedies

Problem: It is far easier for paid circulators to collect enough valid signatures than it is for volunteer-based groups; virtually anyone can qualify an initiative by paying a signature-gathering firm $1–$2+ million.

Remedy: Extend the signature-gathering period well past the current 150 days so that smaller groups have more time to spread their messages and volunteers throughout the state, or ban paid signature gathering.

Problem: Big money dominates the initiative process.

Remedy: Limit campaign donations from groups and individuals. Disclose donor information as close as possible to the date a draft is titled and prominently display that information on initiative petitions and advertising throughout the campaign.

Problem: Ballot measures are confusing and complex.

Remedy: Hold legislative hearings to generate more substantive discussion about a measure's probable impacts, and broadcast them on Web sites and through news media. If two conflicting measures are being considered in the same election, group them together in the ballot pamphlet and explain which will prevail if both pass. In addition, direct voters to online resources to help them in their search for more comprehensive information.

Problem: There are too many initiatives.

Remedy: Require the legislature to vote on proposed laws first. After a public hearing on a measure, the legislature could vote to pass it, with or without any changes that the initiative's authors may approve or reject. Courts could be given a role in verifying that the legislature's version respects the authors' intent.

Problem: It is too difficult to revise initiatives once they become law. They cannot be changed except through a future ballot measure, even if flaws are discovered.

Remedy: Allow the legislature to amend measures after a certain amount of time, holding lawmakers to strict guidelines or further review.

Problem: The state constitution is cluttered with redundant and contradictory amendments.

Remedy: Enable more frequent, comprehensive reviews of the state constitution to weed out obsolete, unnecessary, or contradictory language. Alternatively, require a constitutional revision commission to meet periodically and make recommendations that voters or lawmakers may act upon.

Problem: Too many initiatives are declared unconstitutional.

Remedy: Require that a measure be reviewed at a legislative hearing or by a panel of active or retired judges to determine whether the proposed law is consistent with the California state constitution. Inform voters of any conflicts, and give authors the option to withdraw their measures.

For further reading, see *Democracy by Initiative: Shaping California's Fourth Branch of Government,* 2nd ed. (Los Angeles: Center for Governmental Studies, 2008). Available online at www.cgs.org/images/publications/cgs_dbi_full_book_f.pdf.

to the most recalls (about 75 percent of all recalls are against elected school board members), yet they remain relatively rare events, and the same is true of referenda on local decisions or ordinances. On the other hand, citizens have the power to generate laws and use the process to address all manner of issues with a local flair, and they do so with varying success. Between 2009 and 2010, about half of the 115 different petitions that were circulated in 537 city and county jurisdictions later qualified for the ballot, and more than half of them passed.[6] Local initiatives have imposed term limits on city council members or county supervisors (a more common reform in the past ten years), changed the manner and conduct of elections (for instance, San Francisco now allows Saturday voting), affected utility rates, dictated how land was to be used by private businesses, altered the compensation packages for city employees or officials (eliminating retirement, for example), and touched on every manner of civil rights, liberties, and public morals (marriage, immigration, gambling, alcohol use, marijuana legalization).

Local measures rarely generate much attention or press unless the issue is controversial or deep-pocketed interests are at stake. For example, in 2011 a measure banning male circumcision in San Francisco initially qualified for the fall 2011 (municipal) ballot but was withdrawn after a judge ruled that it violated a state law prohibiting cities from regulating medical practices, and City of Redlands voters in 2010 considered banning big-box retailers such as Wal-Mart from establishing new megastores within city limits. In the latter instance the local activists, who raised and spent about $9,000, lost to the large retailer, which bankrolled $450,000 to defeat the measure.

The procedures for circulating a local initiative are similar to those at the state level and are spelled out in the state's election codes: signature requirements, strict circulation guidelines, signature verification carried out by the county registrar of voters, and certification either by the registrar or the city clerk. Signature requirements vary among cities because they are based on prior turnout (for ordinances or local laws) or voter registration (for charter amendments); thus, it takes about seventy-two hundred signatures to qualify an initiative ordinance in San Francisco, but only forty-five hundred in Murietta, for instance. Unlike the state process, citizens must first file a notice of intent to circulate a petition, and, depending on the number of valid signatures gathered, the local governing board (city council or county supervisors) may first consider and adopt a proposed measure without alteration before it's submitted to voters. Local initiatives are placed on ballots as "Measure [letter]," such as "Measure U," as distinct from state propositions that are assigned numbers. From 2009–2010, only forty-two cities considered one or more local ballot measures (see Figure 3.4).

Conclusion: Frustrating Collective Action

California's unique blend of representative and direct democracy creates winners who use public authority to establish their version of reform and their vision

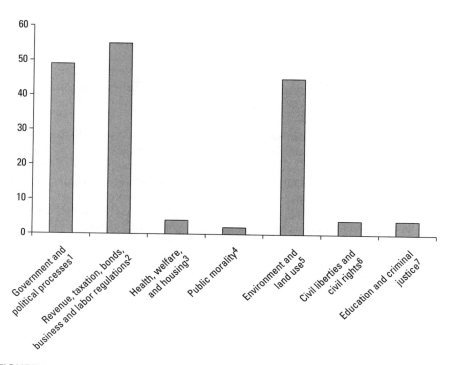

FIGURE 3.4

Subject Matter of Municipal and County Citizen-Proposed Initiatives, 2007–2010

[1] Includes changes to elections, powers of elected officials, appointed versus elected positions, compensation and benefits for public officials and civil service, term limits, districting, and vital city services and administration.

[2] Includes tax rates, utility rates, school bonds, labor contracting, appropriations, and business and labor regulations.

[3] Includes rent control.

[4] Includes medical marijuana dispensaries.

[5] Includes zoning changes, land-use planning, and big-box retail-related measures.

[6] Includes eminent domain and right to buy/sell fireworks.

[7] Includes prohibitions on military recruitment of children.

Note: Measures were reported to the secretary of state on a biannual basis, though a few cities failed to submit reports each year. This count includes only measures that were brought by citizens and excludes recalls and local bond measures placed on the ballots by city councils.

Of ninety-four citizen-initiated measures brought to local California ballots in 2007–2008, the passage rate was 54.3 percent. Of sixty-nine citizen-initiated measures on local ballots in 2009–2010, only forty passed, yielding a 58 percent passage rate.

Source: California Secretary of State, "Report on County Initiative Measures," www.sos.ca.gov/elections/ballot-measures/pdf/county-initiative-09-10.pdf and "Report on Municipal Initiative Measures," www.sos.ca.gov/elections/ballot-measures/pdf/municipal-initiative-09-10.pdf.

of "better" policy that reflects their values and interests. As political devices for creating change, the initiative, referendum, and recall do not encourage the compromises needed to solve dilemmas that frustrate collective action. Unlike bills that pass through many hands and many points where they can be tweaked, reconsidered, adjusted to accommodate concerns, or obstructed, the referendum, recall, and initiative take one unchanging form that demands a simple "yes" or "no" response from voters at one point in time.

Even though voters make far fewer decisions at the ballot box than legislators make in a typical morning, the political, fiscal, and social impacts of initiatives and referenda can profoundly upset the status quo—frequently with unintended consequences. Yet direct democracy is sacred in California. Citizens believe they make better public policy decisions than elected officials do,[7] and voters continually reshape their government with the goal of "making things work." California's hybrid democracy doesn't ensure that things will get better or that government will work more efficiently, but direct democracy feeds citizens' hopes that it will. For better or worse, direct democracy will continue to restructure the relationship between Californians and their government.

Notes

1. The term "hybrid democracy" is attributed to Elizabeth Garrett, "Hybrid Democracy," *George Washington Law Review 73* (August 2005): 1,096.

2. Initiative and Referendum Institute, iandrinstitute.org.

3. Elisabeth Gerber, Arthur Lupia, Mathew D. McCubbins, and D. Roderick Kiewiet. *Stealing the Initiative* (Upper Saddle River, NJ: Prentice Hall, 2001), 12.

4. Public Policy Institute of California, "Just the Facts: Californians and the Initiative Process," November 2008, http://www.ppic.org/content/pubs/jtf/JTF_InitiativeJTF.pdf. Polls conducted September 2008 (2,002 adults) and October 2008 (2,004 adults). Fifty-nine percent agreed with the statement "There are too many propositions on the state ballot." Seventy-eight percent agreed that "ballot wording for citizens' initiatives is often too complicated and confusing for voters to understand what happens if the initiative passes." A combined 64 percent believed that minor or major change is needed in the initiative process.

5. According to the National Conference of State Legislators, "at least 29 states" permit recall elections to be held in local jurisdictions, but it notes that "some sources place this number at 36." See NCSL, "Recall of State Officials," April 5, 2011, http://www.ncsl.org/default.aspx?tabid=16581.

6. By law, figures on local initiatives are reported to the California secretary of state; however, some cities fail to report by the deadline.

7. Public Policy Institute of California, "Just the Facts: Californians and the Initiative Process," November 2008, http://www.ppic.org/content/pubs/jtf/JTF_InitiativeJTF.pdf.

CHAPTER 4

The State Legislature

Should all dogs and cats be sterilized after they reach six months of age? Should parents be granted unrestricted administrative access to their thirteen-year-old's Facebook or other social media accounts, and should companies be penalized if they do not immediately remove unwanted content? Should affordable health care be available to all Californians? Legislators answer just such questions. Throughout the lawmaking process, they are obligated to express the will of the citizens they represent, and they make decisions that touch almost every aspect of people's lives.

Design, Purpose, and Function of the Legislature

In California's system of separated powers, the legislature makes law or policy, the executive branch enforces or implements it, and the judicial branch interprets the other branches' actions. Chapters 2 and 3 discussed how the people also dabble in lawmaking through the initiative process, but legislators are primarily responsible for solving the state's problems. California's full-time lawmakers are far better suited to the task. They grapple with complex issues year-round and are assisted by professional staff members who help assess anticipated outcomes, research the history of similar attempts, evaluate alternatives, and analyze the costs of proposed laws.

BOX 4.1 FAST FACTS on the California Legislature

Lower house:	Assembly, 80 members
Upper house:	Senate, 40 members
Term length:	Assembly, 2 years; senate, 4 years
Term limits:	Assembly, 6 years; senate, 8 years
Majority party in Assembly and Senate:	Democratic
Leaders:	Speaker of the assembly, president pro tem of the senate, minority leaders of the assembly and senate
Leaders' salaries:	$109,584* plus a per diem of $142/day**
Legislators' salaries:	$95,291* plus a per diem of $142/day**

Source: California Citizens Compensation Commission, "Salaries of Elected Officials," October 5, 2010, www.dpa.ca.gov/cccc/salaries/main.htm.

*As determined by the Citizens Compensation Commission, salaries decreased 18 percent effective December 2009, a drop of more than $20,000 per legislator. Salaries did not increase between 2009 and 2012, but in April 2011 legislators' official car allowances were slashed by more than half, to $300 per month.

**Per the senate and assembly rules committees, per diem amounts are set by the Victim Compensation and Government Claims Board and are intended to cover daily expenses associated with working away from home. Total amounts vary annually with the number of days in session and by chamber. The annual average per diem decreased to $31,850 beginning in 2009.

California's legislature resembles the U.S. Congress in both structure and function. Like its federal counterpart, it is bicameral; that is, it is divided into two houses that check each other. Legislators in both the state's eighty-member lower house, called the **assembly**, and the forty-member upper house, the **senate**, represent districts that are among the most populous in the nation: based on the 2010 census, assembly districts average 465,600 people, and senate districts average nearly 931,350 residents.[1]

Unlike members of the U.S. Congress, however, California legislators are term limited. In 1990 voters adopted Proposition 140, a term-limits initiative that restricts assembly members to three two-year terms, for a total of six years, and senators to two four-year terms, or eight years total. Lifetime bans prohibit lawmakers from running for the same offices once they've reached those limits. Prop 140 has profoundly influenced individuals' perspectives and the way the legislature operates, a point revisited later in this chapter.

Legislators are elected from districts that are redrawn once a decade based on the U.S. Census. Redrawing district boundaries has traditionally rested with senate and assembly committees, but Proposition 11 (passed in 2008) handed the mapmaking power over to an independent citizens' commission. Proponents hope this decision will increase party competitiveness and the election of moderates, as well as reduce the power of incumbents.

California Representatives at Work

California's legislature has come a long way from the days when allegiances to the Southern Pacific Railroad earned it the nicknames "the legislature of a thousand steals" and "the legislature of a thousand drinks." Today its members are the highest paid in the nation, earning more than $100,000 per year, including per diem payments intended to cover living costs. Special interests and their lobbyists still permeate Sacramento politics with their presence, money, and messages, but legislators' loyalties these days are splintered by district needs, statewide demands, and partisanship. Crammed schedules are split between their home districts and Sacramento.

Nowadays, term limits create large classes of freshman legislators every two years, pushing others into campaigns for the next office and year-round fundraising. Nearly everyone is on a learning curve, anticipating the next election and aware that the clock is ticking. Rigid ideological positioning has driven Democrats and Republicans to gridlock over raising taxes and cutting social programs—key components of balancing the budget. Often the air seems combustible.

In many ways the legislature is a microcosm of California. More than ever before the demographics of the assembly and senate resemble the state's population (see Figure 4.1). There are more women and ethnic minority members representing

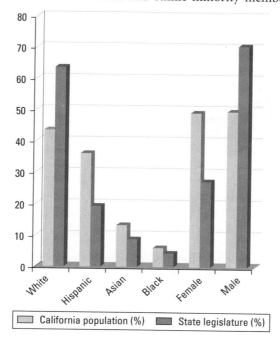

FIGURE 4.1

Profile of California's Population vs. California State Legislature

Sources: Mac Taylor, "CAL Facts," Legislative Analyst's Office, California Department of Finance, (published January 2011); author's data, snapshot of legislature in June 2011.

BOX 4.2 **Term Limits: Political Earthquake**

Have term limits for legislators been good or bad? Both supporters and detractors can find ammunition in the findings. One thing neither side can deny, however, is that the reform has dramatically changed the rules of representation and the environment in which legislators work.

Prior to the passage of Prop 140 in 1990, state legislators were condemned for being out-of-touch careerists who had developed cozy relationships with lobbyists. Observers blamed stagnant rates of member turnover on uncompetitive elections, and the legislature was still reeking from a Federal Bureau of Investigation (FBI) sting two years earlier that had charged fourteen state officials with bribery, including three legislators who went to jail.

The electorate was ready for change when an initiative modeled after one passed shortly before in Oklahoma qualified for the ballot. Echoes of the early California Progressives were heard in proponents' sweeping promises to restore a "government of citizens representing their fellow citizens."* The measure quickly gained momentum and passed with just over 52 percent of the vote. Since then, support for term limits among Californians has solidified and increased, and twenty other states subsequently adopted similar measures, although these were invalidated or repealed in six states, bringing the current total number of states with term limits to fifteen.

Willie Brown, Speaker of the California State Assembly from 1980 to 1995, was an easy target of term-limits supporters for his perceived abuses of power and flashy style.

Term limits had an immediate impact. Long-term legislators were forced to campaign for other elected offices, and staff members were driven into private lobbying firms when Prop 140 slashed legislative budgets. Within a few years, long-standing Speaker Willie Brown was mayor of San Francisco, assembly careers were ending for good, and sitting senators were anticipating their next move. Overall, the wide-ranging effects have touched virtually every aspect of legislative life, and they range from positive to negative.

Electoral Changes

- Competition has increased for political offices at all levels, from county boards of supervisors to seats in the U.S. Congress, as more termed-out legislators run for them.
- Open-seat primary elections occur with regularity and can be ferociously competitive; open-seat general elections in a handful of districts are competitive as well.
- Incumbents still have huge advantages—about 99 percent are reelected. Many cruise to victory without serious challengers, and some face no challengers at all.
- Nearly all senators are former members of the state assembly, and a few will return to the assembly to finish serving out a final term before reaching their lifetime limits (fourteen years: six in the assembly, eight in the senate).
- Intraparty competition has risen as members of the same party vie for the same seats—usually in the state senate.

Membership Changes

- Far higher numbers of open seats have encouraged the candidacies and election of ethnic minority members—higher than would be expected through redistricting alone. More than a third of legislators are Latino, African American, or Asian American.
- Higher turnover has led to record numbers of female candidates for office since 1990, though their total percentage of membership follows a longer historical upward trend unconnected to term limits.
- More women are being elected to the senate and occupy more leadership roles in both houses; these trends are more apparent among Democrats.

Institutional Changes

- Newer legislators have recently experienced the effects of current laws in their districts and have fresh ideas about how to address problems arising from them.
- "Institutional memory" has drained away as career legislators and their staffs leave; members are less expert across a range of policy areas than in the past, and their knowledge of how state systems interrelate is poorer.
- The average senator has about two-and-a-half times as much legislative experience as the average assembly member.
- Senate staff members tend to be more experienced than assembly staff members and consider the upper house the "watchdog" of the more turnover-prone assembly.
- Lobbyists that represent powerful groups, have experience, and are well connected can quickly establish relationships and exert undue influence over legislators. Lobbyists must work harder to get to know those new legislators, however, as they are likely to be regarded with skepticism.
- Executive branch departments command informational resources and benefit from less frequent institutional turnover, rendering oversight by the legislature even more difficult than in the past.

Behavioral Changes

- "Lame duck" legislators lack electoral accountability to their current districts. Many look to their next possible constituency when considering how to vote; some feel less obligated to lobbyists in their last terms and more frequently feel free to "vote their conscience."
- Long-term, comprehensive lawmaking suffers as term-limited legislators lack the time and incentive to tackle many big projects or issues that will outlast their tenures. Smaller district-level projects are more attractive to term-limited legislators.
- There is a sense that "everyone is running for the next office," probably because about two-thirds of legislators will run for another office within two years of being termed out, and most will stay in the public sector.

Sources: Author's data. See also Bruce Cain, Thad Kousser, and Karl Kurtz, "California: A Professional Legislature after Term Limits," in Governing California, Gerald C. Lubenow, ed. (Berkeley: IGS Press, 2006); and Ava Alexandar, "Citizen Legislators or Political Musical Chairs: Term Limits in California." (Los Angeles: Center for California Studies, 2011).

*California Secretary of State, "Argument in Favor of Proposition 140," November 1990 ballot pamphlet.

a wider range of ages and backgrounds, and more than one-third of senate and assembly members identify as an ethnic minority. The extent to which a legislature is, as U.S. Founder John Adams put it, "an exact portrait, in miniature, of the people at large,"[2] is a measure of **descriptive representation**. The extent to which members translate those outward features, as well as their values, into meaningful policies is **substantive representation**.

Policymaking and Lawmaking

Assembly members and senators fulfill their representative functions chiefly through various aspects of lawmaking. To deal with approximately five thousand bills and measures introduced in a two-year session, they gather information through research generated by their staff, they pay attention to the cues given by their colleagues, and they visit sites such as schools and interact with community leaders and citizens to get a better sense of their districts. They introduce bills addressing problems that lobbyists or constituents bring to their attention. As members of committees (where the bulk of policymaking occurs), they help shape or amend legislation after fielding complaints, testimony, and predictions from witnesses who will be affected by potential changes. They deliberate and vote both in committee and later on the assembly or senate floor, where every member has a chance to vote on every bill. As all bills must be passed in identical form by both houses before the governor can veto or sign them, members also continue building support for, or opposition to, measures that are moving through the other house.

Each bill bears the imprint of a unique set of players, is shaped by the rules, and is affected by timing. More often than not, the concerns of important groups are gathered throughout the bill passage process and accommodated to some degree. Legislators tend to be sensitive to the fears and threats expressed by well-financed, vocal, influential, and large organizations that support their party or are active in their districts. For instance, businesses that employ large numbers of people in a legislator's district may be called upon to testify about bills or may be asked to provide feedback about pending legislation.

Relationships also matter. Partisans tend to support fellow partisans, but legislators who get to know others "across the aisle" tend to be more willing to support them legislatively. Because in the final analysis compromise is key, relationships among the players—from legislative staff to legislators to lobbyists to the governor's staff—help facilitate necessary give and take.

Bills vary in scope, cost, urgency, and significance and cover every imaginable topic. Most go no further than being referred to a committee. Of lesser scope and significance are simple **resolutions** passed to express the legislature's position on an issue. For example, in March 2009 the assembly passed a resolution "memorializing its opposition to Proposition 8" on the grounds that the proposition improperly revised the state constitution. No Republican supported the resolution, but it was adopted by a majority vote of Democrats. Inexpensive "**local bills**," which deal with

The Senate Rules Committee holds a hearing to consider the appointment of Mary Nichols to chair the California Air Resources Board (CARB). A former state Department of Resources secretary and chair of CARB under Jerry Brown from 1978–1983, she reassumed the post in 2007 and continues to hold the post in the new Brown administration.

such concerns as specific land uses, may matter a lot to the people directly affected by the legislation but usually have only a minor impact on state government. Many bills relate to the administration of government and make technical changes or amendments to existing state law. These proposed **statutes** might impose mandates, or obligations, on local governments or agencies, such as requiring the governing boards of state colleges and universities to provide for live audio transmission of all public meetings. New laws (statutes) are also needed to authorize public agencies to take on new responsibilities or to collect fees, such as charging individuals a fee for copies of environmental impact reports. Other bills create new categories of crime, authorize commission studies, or set up programs. For example, it takes a law to establish a nature conservancy for the restoration of environmentally sensitive areas or to set up a recovery program for unused paint that might otherwise be illegally dumped.

Legislators also introduce bills that at first glance may appear to make small changes, but which, if enacted into law, will have tangible effects on Californians and their local governments. For instance, as of 2000, city and county governments are supposed to be diverting half of the solid waste generated locally away from landfills; a proposal to make it 60 percent by 2015 would cause cities and counties to revisit this issue and devise new plans to deal with their waste, from

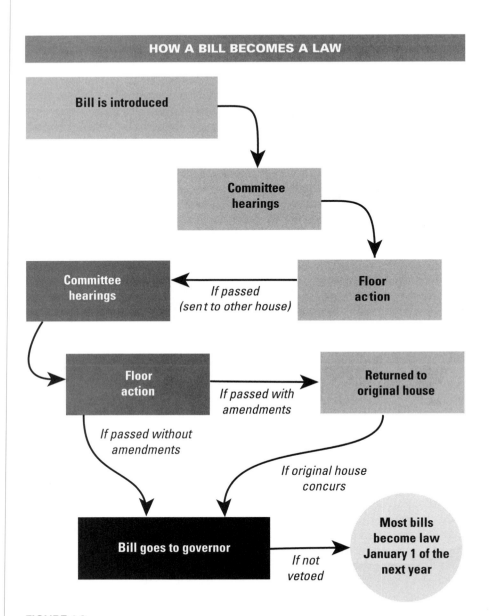

HOW A BILL BECOMES A LAW

Bill is introduced

Committee hearings

Floor action

*If passed
(sent to other house)*

Committee hearings

Floor action

If passed with amendments

Returned to original house

If passed without amendments

If original house concurs

Bill goes to governor

If not vetoed

Most bills become law January 1 of the next year

FIGURE 4.2

How a Bill Becomes a Law

imposing fees to further regulating businesses to trying to change household habits. Of major import are multimillion- or billion-dollar, long-range, complex bills that affect many different groups and usually require years of study and compromise. Examples include revising workers' compensation programs, determining MediCal benefits, or regulating ecosystems like the San Francisco Bay and Delta. Unfortunately, term-limited members lack incentive to unwind knotty problems that take years to understand and for which they will receive little credit, though this does not stop all legislators from trying to "make a difference." Some lobbyists, especially those who have greater longevity and expertise than legislators, help craft solutions to problems that sitting lawmakers do not understand well.

Given the scope and complexity of the state's ongoing issues, legislators need help. Thousands of staff members working in legislators' capitol and district offices or for committees in both chambers assist with scheduling, constituent relations, research, and expert legislative analysis. The senate, which has retained more veteran professional committee staff and more experienced legislators, tends to collectively view itself as having stronger filters for "bad ideas." Staff members are particularly invaluable players in analyzing the thousands of bills that cross legislators' desks during a two-year term.

Legislators also heavily depend on institutional housekeepers like the assembly chief clerk's staff or the senate's secretary to ensure that legislators follow standing rules and parliamentary procedures. The nonpartisan **Legislative Analyst's Office** (**LAO**) has been the so-called conscience and eyes and ears of the legislature since 1941, providing fiscal and policy advice based on continuing, in-depth research of programs, bills, and the annual budget. It remains one of the premier sources of information about state programs and the budget (www.lao.ca.gov). Similarly, since 1913 the nonpartisan **Legislative Counsel** has acted as an in-house law firm, crafting legislators' proposals into formal bills, rendering legal opinions, and making bill information available electronically (www.leginfo.ca.gov).

It should also be noted that the majority party controls the fate of nearly all bills because simple majorities (forty-one in the assembly; twenty-one in the senate) are needed for passage, though a good number of bills are noncontroversial and pass unanimously. The bottom line: minority-party Republicans are at the mercy of majority Democrats when it comes to lawmaking, and their bills rarely move out of committee. Democrats can safely ignore the minority unless they need Republican votes to pass fiscal measures such as new tax or fee hikes that require a two-thirds supermajority.

Annual Budgeting

It takes the legislature more than half the year to work out an annual budget for the fiscal year (FY) that starts July 1. The process formally begins on January 10 when the governor submits his version to the legislature, and it should end by June 15, when the budget is officially due—but long overdue budgets have been the norm for decades. Voters hoped to prod legislators into acting sooner by passing an initiative in 2010 that eliminated salaries and benefits for each day the budget was not passed on time.

During the winter and spring of a normal fiscal year, the committees in both houses divvy up the work of determining how much money is needed to keep

TABLE 4.1   A Day in the Life of Senator Christine Kehoe

July 6, 2011 Wednesday	
All Day	High school intern in capitol office, July 5–7
8:00 am–9:00 am	Lesbian, gay, bisexual, transgender (LGBT) legislative caucus meeting/breakfast, the Grange Restaurant (chair)
9:00 am–9:30 am	FYI: Assembly Committee on Appropriations (Room 4202), SB 801, SB 206, SB 207, SB 328 staff briefing
9:00 am–1:30 pm (note overlaps)	Governance and Finance Committee (Room 112), 33 bills. Special Order of Business, SB781 (disincorporation of City of Vernon, 11:00 am–12:30 pm)
9:15 am–9:45 am	Appropriations briefing with Brendan McCarthy (committee consultant)
9:30 am–10:30 am (note overlaps)	Appropriations (Room 113), ABX1 13 Perez, endangered species: environmental impact reports, & ABX1 14 Skinner, energy upgrade financing
1:00 pm–1:30 pm (note overlaps)	Quick lunch at desk and briefing with staff about upcoming bills
1:30 pm–3:00 pm (note overlaps)	Assembly Committee on Natural Resources (Room 444), SB 436 (land use) and SB 468 (HOV toll lanes)
1:30 pm–3:00 pm (note overlaps)	Committee on Banking and Finance (Room 112), 5 bills
2:00 pm–3:45 pm (note overlaps)	Latino and LGBT caucus health briefing, Room 127 (deliver welcome remarks; co-chairing with Asm. Ricardo Lara)
1:30 pm–4:00 pm (note overlaps)	Environmental Quality Committee (Room 2040), 15 bills; back and forth to Banking and Finance where votes will be held open
4:00 pm–4:30 pm	Call Chris Nichols, *North County Times* re: SB 468, I-5 (Department of Transportation: North Coast Corridor Project: high-occupancy toll lanes)
4:30 pm–5:00 pm	(Meet & greet) new executive director, EQCA (Equality California) Roland Palencia and Mario Guerrero (Atkins office, Room 4146)

government programs running. Big-ticket items such as education are automatically funded, leaving a relatively small chunk of the budget pie for discretionary purposes; therefore, each legislator fights hard for the crumbs. Until recently the inherently partisan process was aggravated by the rule that two-thirds of both the senate and assembly had to approve the budget—a threshold that was lowered via initiative (in 2010) to a simple majority. The change has not eradicated the influence of partisanship, however, because two-thirds approval is still needed to raise taxes and fees, an option that is difficult to avoid without deeply slashing government programs during difficult budget years. Supermajority rules such as this effectively grant tremendous power to a few at the expense of majority rule, because a few minority party members can arm-twist the majority into major concessions in exchange for needed votes.

Constituency Service and Outreach

Constituency service entails "helping constituents navigate through the government system,"[3] particularly when their troubles stem from bureaucratic "red tape." Legislators hire caseworkers to help them respond quickly to requests, and these staff members spend their days tracking down California Department of Transportation (CalTrans) managers and scheduling appointments at state agencies for frustrated constituents, among other things. Legislators take constituency service seriously, although it is not mentioned in the state constitution. Many consider it "paramount to return every phone call, letter, and e-mail" and make government seem friendlier through personal contact.[4]

Most legislators try to communicate frequently with district residents via e-mail, Web sites, or franked mail pieces (correspondence paid for through office budgets). Other activities include addressing select groups like Rotary clubs or attending special public events (store openings, groundbreakings for public facilities, parades, and so forth). This kind of constituent outreach, or "**public relations**" as some members call it, helps educate constituents, helps the representatives get to know their constituents, and provides incumbents with necessary ammunition for reelection by enhancing their name recognition and reputations.

Executive Branch Oversight

Who monitors programs to ensure that a law is being carried out according to the legislature's intent? Ideally, assembly members, senators, and their staff should be systematically reviewing programs and questioning administrators by having them appear as witness in committee hearings, but term-limited legislators have little time or staff resources to determine if the laws they have created are being faithfully executed. In practice, they rely on investigative reports in the media, lobbyists, citizens, and administrators to sound the alarm about needed fixes. Once a problem is identified, the assembly and senate can rescue legislative intent by threatening to reduce program funding or eliminate the positions of uncooperative state employees. Senators also influence programs through the power to confirm gubernatorial appointees to boards and commissions, such as the Air Resources Board or the Department of Corrections.

The assembly floor is normally a beehive of activity when the house is in session. A view from the rear of the chamber shows Republican members' desks on the left-hand side and Democratic members' desks on the right (from the Speaker's view the Democrats are seated to the left and Republicans to the right, reflecting their traditional ideological placement). Members cast votes by pressing buttons on their desk, and votes are registered on digital display boards at the front of the chamber.

Leaders

Aside from the governor, the Speaker of the assembly and the president pro tem of the senate are among the most powerful figures in Sacramento. Along with the governor and the minority leaders of each house, these individuals form the "Big Five" of California government: the leaders who speak for all their fellow party members in their house and are ultimately responsible for cobbling together last-minute political bargains that clinch the budget or guarantee the signing of big bills.

A party leader's job is to keep his or her majority in power or to regain majority status. Nonstop fund-raising, policymaking, rulemaking, and dealmaking all serve that overarching objective. Party leaders oversee their *caucus* (all the members of a party in one house) and help shape the electorate's understanding of what it means to support a "Democratic" or "Republican" agenda. Still, institutional agendas are fluid and more often than not they emerge from commonalities among legislators' individual designs more than they are imposed by elites at the top. However, the general rule is: what leadership wants, leadership gets. Leaders' ability to obtain desired results rests on many factors, including having credible weapons such as the power to remove members from choice committees. They may also endorse opponents, cut off campaign funds, reduce office budgets midyear, or move offices or parking spaces to undesirable locations. For instance, Assemblyman Anthony Portantino's office budget was slashed in summer 2011 after he cast the only Democratic vote against the state budget bill.

The Speaker is the most visible member of the assembly and its spokesperson at-large. He or she negotiates budgets, bills, and policies on behalf of the entire membership; curries a high profile with the press; and cultivates a distinct culture of discipline and institutional independence through a unique and personal leadership style. Leaders actively use the campaign funds they raise to reward faithful party members and punish traitors. The senate's president pro tem plays these same roles, and in a term-limited era when legislative experience is concentrated in the senate, the senate leader's visibility has increased relative to that of the Speaker.

Speakers appoint chairs and members to all assembly committees, as does the president pro tem through his or her chairing of the all-powerful, five-member Rules Committee. Given that most senators are former assembly members, committees in the upper house are chaired not by freshmen or sophomores with zero to five years' legislative experience (as they are in the lower house) but usually by members who have been in the legislature at least four years when seated. The president pro tem also can use the Rules Committee's power over the governor's key administrative appointments as a bargaining chip in budget and bill negotiations—a tool the Speaker lacks.

Democratic senate president pro tem Darrell Steinberg (left) confers with Republican senate minority leader Bob Dutton in June 2011 as the state senate prepares to debate the annual budget.

The battle to replace Assembly Speaker Karen Bass (center) was resolved when top contender Kevin DeLeón conceded to colleague John Pérez, who became the first openly gay Speaker in California history in 2010. Speakers today share the limelight with the usually more-experienced senate president pro tem.

These days neither the Speaker nor the senate president pro tem regularly leads floor sessions. Visitors catch glimpses of them as they crisscross the floor to privately speak with members in an effort to find support for bills and negotiate deals while normal business proceeds. More often than not, a colleague acting as an assistant "pro tem" guides floor proceedings.

Leaders never forget that they are chosen by colleagues and stay only as long as they can maintain their trust and confidence by meeting their political needs. This was as true for flashy former Speaker Willie Brown (1980–1995) as it is for Speakers today. No tyrants can survive, if only because so many potential replacements impatiently wait in the wings—and under term limits, they needn't wait long before the next opportunity arises. Brown presided over the assembly for almost fifteen years. In the span of fifteen years following his departure there were *ten* Speakers.

Conclusion: Of the People, for the People

Although the legislature's basic framework has changed little since the constitutional revision of 1879, major changes in electoral law, campaign finance rules, ethics law, redistricting, compensation levels, and terms of office have molded and remolded California's legislative environment. Initiatives continue to complicate the already difficult task of condensing a multitude of competing interests, opinions, backgrounds, values, expectations, and ideas into an effective decision-making body. Californians have been quick to alter the political rules to make their representatives resistant to what is generally regarded as the poisonous influence of partisanship, money, and power, yet they have done so with limited success.

Lawmaking is *supposed* to be hard, and an institution that features overlapping powers and shared responsibilities among many elected officials inevitably frustrates it. In California the policymaking process is further complicated by direct democracy and hyperdiversity. Bills bear the imprints of competing interest groups, parties, leaders, funding sources, personal ambitions, rules, history, and a host of other factors that influence choice and impede the easy resolution of issues. Short of creating a tyranny, no reform will change that.

The California state legislature comes closest to the U.S. Congress in form than any other in the nation. Perhaps that is one reason for its dismal approval ratings, but it also remains the best hope for each citizen to achieve a degree of representation that would be unimaginable under an unelected bureaucracy, a dictatorial governor, or even a part-time legislature responsible for helping to govern one of the largest "countries" on the globe. The lawmaking body is closer to the people than the other two branches could ever be: neither the elected executives nor judges can understand the needs and interests of California's communities as thoroughly as firmly anchored representatives can. Not enough attention is paid to the hundreds of public-spirited men and women who have served and are serving resolutely and honorably as California state legislators—individuals who work hard to sustain representative democracy.

Notes

1. The U.S. Census 2000 apportionment population in congressional districts is 646,952; California contains fifty-three U.S. House districts. Data available at http://nationalatlas.gov/articles/boundaries/a_conApport.html.

2. Quoted in Hannah Pitkin, *The Concept of Representation* (Berkeley: University of California Press, 1967), 60.

3. Donald Lathbury, "Two-Thirds Majority Battle Still on Radar," The California Majority Report, September 22, 2008, www.camajorityreport.com/index.php?module=articles&func=display&ptid=9&aid=3581.

4. Author's interview with freshman assembly member in Sacramento, California, in March 1999.

The Executive Branch

Question: Who is in charge of California's K–12 education system?

Answer: Although the *governor* guides education policy through budgetary changes and is often held responsible for the overall state of education, it is the elected *state superintendent of public instruction* who heads the system by constitutional mandate, overseeing the *Department of Education*, the agency through which the public school system is regulated and controlled as required by law, taking cues from the administration's powerful *State Board of Education*, also appointed by the governor but technically administered by the superintendent, who in turn implements the educational regulations of the State Board of Education . . . not to mention the *assembly* and *senate education committees* that steer education bills into law.

Confusing? A case of checks and balances gone awry? Somewhere among the governor's need to obtain information and make recommendations, the legislature's regulatory imperative, and the people's desire to elect at least one accountable officer, the system evolved into a tangled network of authority that even Department of Education employees have difficulty explaining.

BOX 5.1 FAST FACTS on California's Plural Executive

Number of executives:	8, plus the Board of Equalization (12 persons)
Elected executive offices:	Governor Lieutenant governor (LG) Attorney general (AG) Secretary of state Controller Treasurer Superintendent of public instruction Insurance commissioner Board of Equalization (4 of 5 members are elected)
Balance of political parties:	2 Republicans, 9 Democrats, 1 nonpartisan (2010 elections)
Governor's salary:	$173,987*
Salary for AG and superintendent:	$151,127*
Salary for controller, treasurer, and insurance commissioner:	$139,189*
Salary for secretary of state, LG, and Board of Equalization members:	$130,490*
Terms of office:	Four years
Term limits:	Two terms (lifetime ban**)

Source: California Citizens Compensation Commission, "Salaries of Elected Officials," October 5, 2010, www.dpa.ca.gov/cccc/salaries/main.htm.

*A salary decrease of 18 percent went into effect in December 2009; the average decrease was more than $30,000 per official.

**Once an executive has served two terms in a particular office, he or she may not run for that office again. Term limits took effect with Proposition 140 in 1990. Anyone who served prior to 1990 was not prevented from running again; this includes Governor Jerry Brown, who served two terms as governor from 1975 to 1983.

California's Plural Executive

Founders of the United States rejected the notion that more than one person could effectively lead an executive branch. They argued that only one, the president, could bring energy to an office that would otherwise be fractured by competing ambitions and differences of opinion. What then are we to make of California's plural executive, comprised of eight constitutional executive officers plus a five-member board, sharing responsibility for administering state government—the longest list among the states? Or the fact that among them are both Republicans and Democrats?

Term limits on each office—two four-year terms under Proposition 140—also call into question executives' ability or desire to cooperate. As term-limited

Under term limits individuals may only be elected to the same seat twice. Elected officials are usually looking for another job long before eight years are up, and open statewide offices are attractive options to those who have campaigned statewide and have run other aspects of state government. In a term-limited era, it's all about the "next" office.

FIGURE 5.1

California Executives and Musical Chairs

A bold frame indicates these executives served as elected legislators in either or both the assembly and senate.

Note: Debra Bowen lost a bid for a congressional seat in 2011.

colleagues, they are potential or actual rivals for each others' seats, driven from one elected position to the next as in a game of musical chairs. However, despite their responsibilities to lead the nation's most densely populated state jointly, like most elected officials they remain virtually anonymous to average residents.

The duty of an executive is to carry out laws and policies. Whereas federal administrators direct agencies in their departments to implement a coherent presidential agenda, in California a wide assortment of departments, agencies, and commissions serve different masters: the governor, other California executives, the legislature, the entities they are supposed to regulate, or a combination of any of the above. Years of legislative and administrative turf battles, as well as citizen-driven initiatives, have produced a thicket of offices, boards, agencies, and commissions, some of which retain independent regulatory power and many more of which follow the governor's lead. In theory, the dispersion of power across several offices inoculates government against the worst effects of a single, inept leader, but practically speaking, a fragmented power structure works against the production of consistent government policy and counteracts accountability.

California's Governor

According to the state constitution, "The supreme executive power of this State is vested in the Governor," which places him or her first among equals—for none of the elected executive officers answer directly to the governor. The most recognized and powerful figure in California's state government possesses constitutional duties much like those of most other state governors; what distinguishes the office is both the size and hyperdiversity of the constituency (the entire state population) and the resulting volume of conflicts to address.

The usual route to office is through a battering election that commands national headlines. Only former governor Arnold Schwarzenegger initially escaped primary and general election contests, as well as an extended campaign, by winning office through a recall election, replacing Gray Davis, who was a mere one year into his second term. Strong partisans and vigorous fundraisers tend to survive the regular winnowing process, and prior elected experience also tends to be favored—qualities that boosted Jerry Brown to victory in 2010 over his opponent, eBay cofounder Meg Whitman. Brown gained the seat for the second time, having served as governor (1975–1983, prior to the imposition of term limits), secretary of state, mayor of Oakland, and attorney general.

Head of State

A governor has responsibilities both formal and informal. The role of **head of state** resonates with average citizens: the governor appears at official ceremonies and public events, summarizes California's outlook and his or her agenda in an annual "State of the State" address, receives and entertains foreign dignitaries, and speaks for Californians on the national political stage. He also functions as the state's official liaison to federal officials in Washington, DC, and works with other state governors to advance causes nationally.

Chief Executive

The power to execute or carry out the law rests with the governor. The governor indirectly controls the bureaucracy through approximately 850 top-level appointments to his or her cabinet, key administrative posts, and his or her own staff, which numbers about eighty-five individuals—a total reduction of more than 15 percent after Brown took office. These persons put into practice the governor's vision of good governance through the daily decisions they make about thousands of issues. The governor also appoints members to 320 state boards and commissions with more than 2,250 slots to be filled. Examples include advisory groups, boards that manage county fairs, professional licensing bureaus, and specialized councils that deal with everything from marine fisheries to the arts to sex offenders. Appointments to about one hundred full-time administrative positions and seventy-five boards and commissions require senate approval, and overall only a fraction of appointees serve at the governor's whim. For instance, civil service laws protect virtually all state employees, and roughly 99 percent are hired based on merit rather than nepotism, favoritism, or patronage.[1] Outside of this, on rare occasion the governor may name a replacement to an open U.S. Senate seat and has the power to appoint appellate court justices who must be confirmed by a judicial commission and are later subject to voter approval at a retention election (see chapter 6). The governor may also issue **executive orders** directing state employees in how to implement the law, but the governor's power falls short of forcing all elected executives—constitutional partners such as the controller or attorney general—to do his or her bidding.

Faced with a massive budget deficit of over $25 billion and hoping to gather votes for his budget proposal, newly elected governor Jerry Brown took the unprecedented step of appearing before a joint legislative budget committee, where he argued his case and answered questions from legislators on February 24, 2011.

Legislative Powers

Legislatively, the governor plays a significant role by **setting policy priorities** for California not only through proposed laws, but also through the budget. The power to **call special legislative sessions and special elections**, combined with long-term, permanent staff members dedicated to research and program oversight, give the governor's office significant institutional advantages over the legislature.

Aides monitor bills at all stages of the legislative process, from proposing them to participating in critical final negotiations over a bill's wording and price tag. They testify before assembly or senate committees about pending measures and help build coalitions of support or opposition among legislators, interest groups, and other stakeholders. They also advise the governor to **veto** or **sign** legislation, as a bill becomes law after twelve days without gubernatorial action. Like governors in four out of five states, the hand of the governor of California is strengthened by the **line-item veto**, the power to reduce or eliminate dollar amounts in bills or the budget. Governor Schwarzenegger, for example, used the power to eliminate nearly $1 billion in spending from the 2010 budget; Governor Brown immediately vetoed approximately $270 million from the budget the following year (primarily from transportation funds). Veto overrides of such spending items or any bill passed by the legislature are rarely attempted or successful.

Budgeting Power

Budgeting power arguably gives the administration a powerful advantage over the assembly and senate. The **Department of Finance (DOF),** a permanent clearing-house for state financial and demographic information, works in tandem with the governor to propose a budget in January each year and to revise it in May based on actual tax receipts. The nearly 425 employees of this "superdepartment" work year-round to prepare the following year's budget and enact the previous year's financial plan, and they also analyze any legislation that has a fiscal impact.

Chief of Security

The governor promotes security as **commander in chief** of the state's National Guard, which may be called on at short notice to, for example, deliver emergency services to victims of natural disasters. The State Military Reserve is the defense force placed under exclusive control of the governor; the land-based California Army National Guard and Air National Guard dedicated to cyberspace, space, and air capabilities provide support. With few restraints the governor also can pardon, grant clemency, or commute sentences, even for death row inmates. Such reprieves and the reasons for them must be reported to the legislature and are not uncommon. Just before leaving office, Governor Schwarzenegger granted eight pardons and one conditional pardon, and he attracted intense criticism for showing favoritism when he reduced the sentence of a convicted murderer who happened to be the son of close associate and former assembly Speaker Fabian Nuñez.

Party Leader

Finally, a typical governor symbolically heads his or her state **party**. The extent to which a governor can influence fellow party members in state government depends on the governor's commitment to core party principles, however; a conservative such as Governor Pete Wilson (1991–1999) exerted far greater leadership within the California Republican Party than a moderate Republican like Arnold Schwarzenegger ever could, as Schwarzenegger alienated fellow partisans by working with Democrats and staking out policies that defied the state party's official platform.

Sources of Power

The California governor's powers resemble those of U.S. presidents but with important exceptions. The state's constitution limits a governor's ability to live up to citizens' expectations. For example, as the most visible and recognizable leader, the governor sets policy priorities, yet shares responsibility for day-to-day administration with almost a dozen other elected executive officers who may choose not to follow his or her priorities. The governor will still be held to account for his or her actions that condition the overall state of affairs. To overcome this structural disadvantage, the governor must draw on other sources of power to be effective. Some will be institutional, such as whether the governor's party holds a majority in both the assembly and senate, as well as the numerical advantage of the majority. Another factor is the cohesiveness of parties in the legislature, because the presence of many moderates may make the governor's job of reaching compromises much easier, whereas rigid partisans may be unwilling to budge from their positions. Other sources are personal or informal: charisma, the power to persuade, the perception of having a mandate, or strategic use of the media can go a long way in enhancing a governor's power base.

The Constitutional Executive Officers

Should the governor leave the state at any time, the **lieutenant governor** (LG) takes temporary control; should the governor resign, retire early, die, become disabled, or be impeached, the lieutenant governor takes the oath of office. Topping the LG's lackluster list of duties is presiding over the senate, which in practice means exercising a rare tie-breaking vote. The "governor-in-waiting" also sits on the State Lands Commission and several other boards ex officio, or by virtue of his or her position.

Second in power to the governor is actually the **attorney general** (AG), known as the state's chief law enforcement officer. Through the state's Department of Justice, the AG employs deputy attorneys general to help represent the people of California in court cases, provides legal counsel to state officials, coordinates statewide narcotics enforcement efforts, enforces state firearms and gambling laws, assists with criminal investigations, provides forensic science services, and supervises all sheriffs, police chiefs, and state agencies to enforce the law adequately and uniformly. The office is inherently political not only because the state's lead lawyer is elected and may use the position as a stepping stone to bigger and better offices (AG is also shorthand for "*Aspiring Governor*") but also because he or she privileges some causes above others. For example, an AG might step up lawsuits against repeat environmental polluters or sue cities to overturn local ordinances that violate state law.

The **secretary of state** acts as the chief elections officer and oversees all aspects of federal and state elections. This includes registering voters, distributing ballot pamphlets in seven languages, printing ballots, certifying the integrity of voting machines, compiling election results, and publishing election results on the Web and in print. The office's Political Reform Division implements rules relating to proper disclosure of lobbying and campaign activity and makes that information available electronically (www.cal-access.ca.gov). As keeper of official historical records, the secretary of state also charters corporations and nonprofits, maintains business filings, and safeguards the state archives.

Fragmentation of authority is most evident in the three separate offices that regulate the flow of money through the state government. The prominent **controller** (known as comptroller in other states) pays the state's bills and continually monitors the state's financial situation. State employees and vendors who sell services or goods to the state might recognize the controller's signature on their checks. The controller is the at-large member of the State Board of Equalization and sits on numerous advisory boards, including the Tax Franchise Board, which administers personal income and corporate tax laws, and more than sixty other commissions and organizations relating to state payouts such as employee pensions and construction projects.

The second money officer is the **treasurer**, the state's banker who manages the state's investments, assets, and bond debt. Every year the state borrows several billion dollars to finance huge projects such as the rebuilding of bridges or schools, and this borrowing takes the form of bonds sold to investors. The treasurer manages the state's mountainous debt by selling and repaying bonds on an ongoing basis, trying to secure acceptable credit ratings that lead to lower loan interest rates, and maintaining the state's financial assets. The treasurer also chairs or sits on almost sixty boards that are authorized to raise and spend money on huge infrastructure concerns such as rail and road transportation, building and repairing schools, ensuring clean and available water, and housing.

The **Board of Equalization** represents the third money office and consists of the state controller and four other officials elected from districts containing more than nine million Californians apiece. The board's job is to standardize the tax systems in the state, which bring in almost $50 billion per year—nearly

Next to the governor, the most powerful executive officer in California is the attorney general. Here Attorney General Kamala Harris views firearms seized from persons possessing them illegally. In one six-week sweep, Department of Justice officers seized twelve hundred guns. Some of these were taken from persons determined to be mentally unstable or who had active restraining orders against them.

half of the state's general fund revenues in 2009–2010—as well as administer revenue-generating, fee-based programs that generate another 35 percent of the state's annual revenues.[2] Aided by fifty-eight elected county tax assessors, the board ensures that residents pay fair rates on properties, and it also collects state sales and use fees, as well as liquor, tobacco, and fuel excise taxes that fund essential state services. The board is the only one of its type elected in the fifty states, and was evenly split between two Republicans and two Democrats after the 2010 elections.

In the same anti-tax spirit of Proposition 13, voters rebelled against spiraling auto insurance rates and elevated the **Office of Insurance Commissioner** from a governor-appointed subagency to a full-scale executive office in 1988. The elected commissioner is authorized to review and pre-approve rates for car and homeowners' (property and casualty) insurance, grant licenses for agents and companies operating in California, investigate fraudulent practices, and enforce rulings against violators. In recent years the department has taken a stronger role in reviewing health insurance rate increases as well.

As noted in this chapter's opener, the **superintendent of public instruction** leads the Department of Education and advocates for student achievement as the state's only nonpartisan executive officer. The superintendent is the point person for statewide student testing and reporting, including implementation of the state's high school exit exams; data collection on a range of education-related issues such as drop-out rates, yearly funding levels for K–12 and community college education, and student achievement levels; and implementation of the federal No Child Left Behind Act and related federal education policy initiatives.

Though these executive officers are free to consult each other and frequently find themselves in each other's company, at no point do they meet as a governing board, and no mechanism exists to centrally coordinate their work. Sometimes this arrangement makes for strange bedfellows, as Governor Schwarzenegger found in 2009 when he wrote an executive order closing state offices two Fridays per month, effectively furloughing all state workers, including the staff of his fellow executives. However, his mandate legally could not apply to his colleagues, who promptly ignored the order. Sharp disagreements over how to govern during a budget crisis also surfaced between Schwarzenegger and the state's controller, John Chiang, with regard to the issue of temporary pay cuts for state workers. Chiang refused to slash state worker pay to the federal minimum wage level at the governor's request, balking at the logistical nightmare of recalculating paychecks and also shying away from alienating public employee unions, which vehemently opposed the cuts. The contest opened a legal battle over who has the authority to set state workers' pay, and it was ultimately resolved in the governor's favor. One lesson to be gleaned from this example is that an organizational structure that allows Democrats and Republicans to share executive power virtually guarantees that differences in governing philosophies and approaches will exist, but it usually takes a looming crisis to make those differences visible and put them to the test.

Administrators and Regulators

A great checkerboard of departments, administrative offices, boards, and agencies form the state's bureaucracy. Almost all are linked to the governor through the cabinet secretaries whom he or she designates to head each department. All the departments and state agencies these secretaries lead are organized either by statute or initiative and are designed to help the governor execute state law faithfully.

Bureaucratic reorganization occurs periodically, but the "superagency" scheme of Governor Pat Brown—not to be confused with his son, Governor Jerry Brown—has stuck since the 1970s. These superagencies act as umbrella organizations for the smaller departments, boards, and commissions nested within them. The seven superagencies include: (1) Business, Transportation, and Housing; (2) Natural Resources; (3) Youth and Adult Corrections and Rehabilitation; (4) State

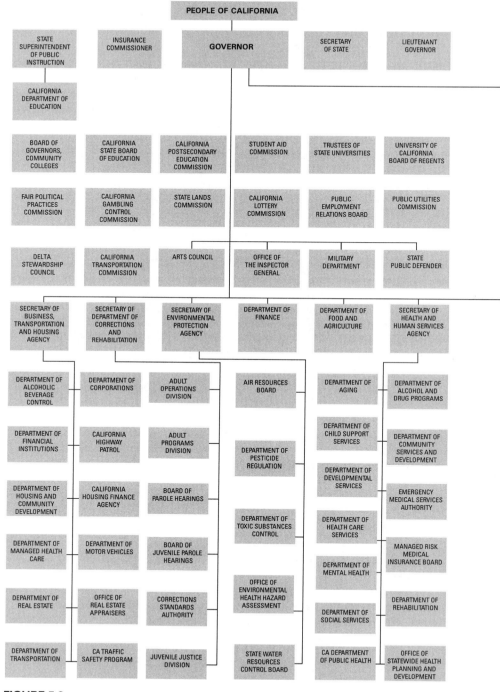

FIGURE 5.2
Organization Chart of California's Executive Branch

THE EXECUTIVE BRANCH

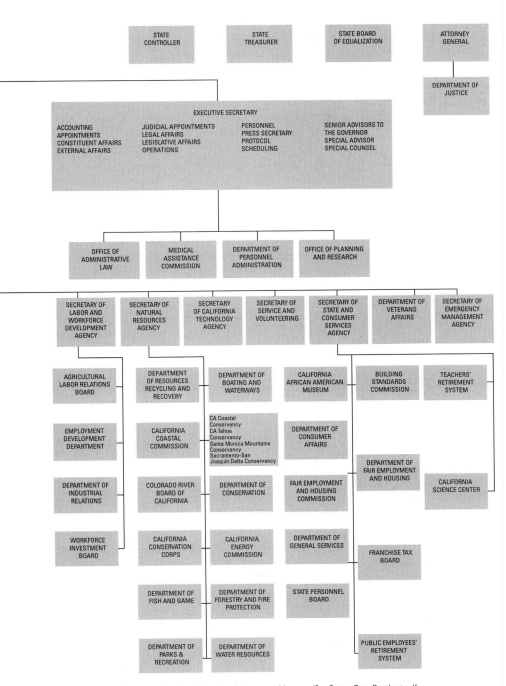

Source: Adapted from organizational chart found at www.cold.ca.gov/Ca_State_Gov_Orgchart.pdf.

Note: Updated July 26, 2011.

and Consumer Services; (5) Health and Human Services; (6) Environmental Protection (EPA), and (7) Labor and Workforce Development. For example, the Business, Transportation, and Housing Department houses twelve entities, including CalTrans, the Department of Motor Vehicles (DMV), and the state highway patrol. Alternatively, the state EPA oversees the Air Resources Board and four other major offices that regulate or assess pesticides, toxic substances, water resources, and other health hazards. Secretaries of these seven superagencies plus remaining departments, including several "superdepartments" that employ many specialists—the Departments of Finance; Food and Agriculture; and Veterans Affairs (see Figure 5.2)—comprise the governor's cabinet. Working for them are just over 232,000 full- and part-time public employees who make up the state bureaucracy—a workforce that decreased nearly 10 percent from 2009 to 2011. Governor Brown eliminated several departments in 2011 to help close the budget gap.[3]

The governor's stamp is also present in membership appointments to some 320 commissions and boards that share regulatory authority with him or her. Among these are large entities such as the University of California's Board of Regents and the State Lands Commission and smaller ones such as the boards overseeing professional licensing for nurses, accountants, and so forth. Most boards consist of four or five members and some meet only twice a year. Full membership turnover of a board rarely occurs during a governor's term; thus, competing ideological viewpoints are often represented on boards depending on who appointed whom. Together, these unelected authorities make rules affecting Californians in virtually every imaginable way, from making beaches accessible to determining trash dump locations.

Conclusion: Competition for Power

The Progressives' lack of faith in parties and mistrust of elected officials have left a legacy of many individuals at the top both sharing and competing for power. Ironically, although no single person is in charge, most Californians believe the governor is and blame him or her when things go awry. Perhaps not surprisingly, then, they are also unwilling to vest more power in that office and have, for example, rejected proposals to allow the governor to cut the budget more easily.[4]

What are we to make, then, of California's plural executive? In the first place, the division of labor among high-profile officials can mean that each brings a different kind of energy and focus to his or her specialized role. The splintering of authority among many offices also provides checks against the concentration of authority, but, perversely, this arrangement also obscures accountability. Decentralized decision making means that voters cannot hold anyone but the governor accountable for decisions produced at the state level, even though he or she may not be the source of their discontent.

In the second place, no one is truly "in charge" of the state, and fragmented authority places limitations on the governor's ability to coordinate a political agenda. The governor may be vested with "supreme" administrative authority by the constitution, but he or she can no more tell the controller what to do than the secretary of state can. State executives are entitled to their own approaches, initiatives, and budgets, and they have little incentive to set aside their ideological differences. Coherent, consistent policy planning does not occur, and Republicans and Democrats continue their work in spite of each other.

For the most part, however, California's executive officers coexist in pursuit of the same basic goal: to allow the state to prosper. Their inability to do so signals just how intractable California's problems are and how the current division of powers complicates the job of finding clear solutions; in other words, it is another measure of how ungovernable the state has become.

Notes

1. Most state workers are members of the powerful union known as the California State Employees Association.

2. California State Board of Equalization, "The Agency and its History," 2009, www.boe .ca.gov/info/agency_history.htm.

3. Total number is 232,149 as of August 2011, including part-time workers and excluding employees of California State Universities. Source: State Controller's Office, "State Employee Demographics," August 2011, www.sco.ca.gov/ppsd_empinfo_demo.html.

4. The most recent examples are Proposition 76 in January 2006 and Proposition 1A in May 2009, both of which were resoundingly defeated.

The Court System

T he state courts' place in a separated system of powers is to verify that the actions of the executive and legislative branches—and also popular will as expressed in initiatives—are lawful and, more generally, to provide "fair and equal access to justice for all Californians."[1] Impartiality forms the judicial system's core, but the branch is political nevertheless. Progressives realized this when they established nonpartisan elections for judges in 1911, but there is no avoiding the fact that many judges must run retention campaigns that can be expensive and further politicized when outspoken donors or independent spenders try to influence election outcomes. Moreover, judges are appointees who make policy through their interpretation of laws and their choices about how to apply them.

California's court system is the largest in the nation, with over twenty-one hundred judicial officers and twenty-one thousand court employees handling over *ten million* cases annually. The state's constitution guarantees citizens the right to a jury trial for both criminal and civil cases, but chronic underfunding has led to overworked employees, shortages of judges, huge trial backlogs, and long delays for those who bring lawsuits—not to mention severe jail overcrowding. The judicial branch is withering from the largest reduction in funding in state history—$350 million for 2011–2012—which came on the heels of a $200 million cutback imposed only a few months earlier. What Chief Justice Tani Cantil-Sakauye has called "devastating and crippling"[2] cuts will translate into regular court closures, fewer employees, extraordinarily long waits in line, and further delays for the millions of people who rely on the courts to deliver justice.[3]

The Three-Tiered Court System

As in the federal judicial system, California courts are organized into three tiers, and the legislature controls the number of judgeships. At the lowest level are trial courts, also called superior courts, which are located in all fifty-eight counties. More than sixteen hundred judges and four hundred commissioners and referees work in the courts at this level. Virtually all ten million cases begin here and are categorized as either criminal or civil. Individuals are tried for three types of crime: felonies, which are serious and possibly violent offenses; misdemeanors, or lesser crimes; and minor infractions for which fines are imposed, including traffic violations, which make up about 60 percent of the superior courts' docket.

Civil suits, on the other hand, involve disputes between individuals or organizations seeking monetary compensation for damages usually incurred through

The California Supreme Court hears arguments regarding the constitutionality of voter-approved Proposition 8, a measure defining marriage as between a man and a woman. The court decided in May 2009 to uphold the law, effectively denying homosexuals the right to wed, but it ruled that the approximately seventeen thousand same-sex unions already performed in the state would remain legal.

injuries, breaches of contract, or defective products. The huge number of civil lawsuits in the state, about 1.7 million annually,[4] reflects a general acceptance of litigation as a "normal" way to resolve problems. The state attorney general can also bring civil cases against companies that break environmental, employment, or other types of state law.

Juvenile, family, and probate cases are also heard in superior court. A single judge or trial juries may decide cases at this level, and persons who cannot afford to pay an attorney are entitled to help with their defense in the form of a public defender.

If the losing party in a case believes the law was not applied properly, he or she may ask the next-higher district **court of appeal** to hear the case. There are no trials in district appellate courts, although three-judge panels may opt to hear lawyers argue a case. Spread across nine court locations are 105 appellate justices who review approximately twenty-four thousand cases for errors, improprieties, or technicalities that could lead to a reversal of the lower court's judgment, though more than half are disposed of without a written opinion. On the whole, appellate court

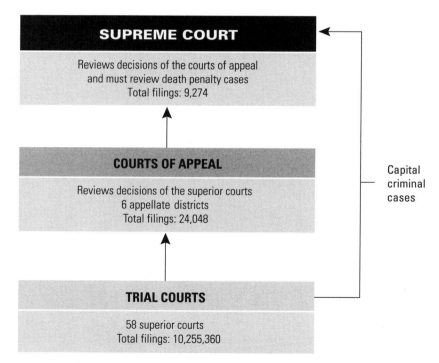

FIGURE 6.1

California Court System

Sources: "California Courts: The Judicial Branch of California," www.courtinfo.ca.gov/courts/about.htm; and Court Statistics Report 2010, http://www.courts.ca.gov/documents/csr2010.pdf.

decisions clarify and actually establish government policy, as the state supreme court allows the great majority of these decisions to stand.

The highest judicial authority is vested in a seven-member **supreme court,** whose decisions are binding on all California courts. Headquartered in San Francisco, justices also hear oral arguments in Los Angeles and Sacramento about cases appealed from the intermediate-level district courts throughout the year, but they automatically review death row cases and exercise original jurisdiction over a few other types. Of roughly ninety-two hundred cases appealed to it in 2008–2009, the court issued a mere 116 written opinions, made available to the public on the court's website (www.courts.ca.gov) and through published official reports. Justices are not required to review all cases and therefore have wide discretion over case selection, concentrating mostly on those that either address important questions of law or promote uniform judgments across the system. They spend considerable time choosing cases, and each justice has numerous support staff and permanent staff attorneys to assist him or her. As the principal supervisor of the lower courts, the chief justice shoulders more responsibility than the other justices. The court's reputation at a given time reflects its collective policy decisions, both in the questions chosen to be addressed or ignored and the court's interpretation of a law's wording and intent.

Appointed by Governor Schwarzenegger in January 2011 to replace retiring Chief Justice of the State Supreme Court Ronald George, Tani Gorre Cantil-Sakauye is the first Asian-Filipina American and the second woman to serve as the state's chief justice. Prior to being elevated to the court's highest position, she served for over two decades on California appellate and trial courts. She also served as a district attorney and on staff for Governor George Deukmejian.

Controversy often stems from the supreme court's review of initiatives, political measures that can only be ruled on after passage and are often overturned in whole or in part for violating the state constitution. Proposition 8, a constitutional amendment that eliminated same-sex marriage by legalizing marriage between a man and a woman only, became a hot potato in 2009 for the justices who were threatened with recall if they overturned it. (They didn't, though three supreme court justices in Iowa who had legalized same-sex marriages were ousted by that state's voters in 2010.)

On and Off the Court

An attorney who has practiced law in California for at least ten years may become a judge, but these individuals usually enter the position through gubernatorial appointment rather than by first running for office. Interested applicants may apply through the governor's office. A governor has ample opportunity to shape the long-term ideological bent of the judiciary by selecting individuals whose partisanship and political principles are reflected in their judicial philosophy. When George Deukmejian (1982–1991) was asked why he was running for governor he replied, "Attorney generals don't appoint judges. Governors do."[5] Governor Arnold Schwarzenegger was far less partisan in his judicial appointments than his predecessors, with just over half Republican, about a third Democrat, and the remainder undeclared.[6] Governors also directly affect the demographic composition of the bench, which today remains disproportionately male, middle class, and white—in contrast to the state's heavily ethnic prison population (see Table 6.1 and Box 6.1). Between November 2003 and December 2010, Governor Schwarzenegger made 627 appointments to the bench.

Superior court justices serve for six years without term limitations, and if they were first appointed to office and not elected, they must become nonpartisan candidates for their office when their term expires. Longer terms are intended to increase the judiciary's independence and consistency over time by reducing the frequency of distracting campaigns that can create potential conflicts of interest with campaign contributors. Contested elections are rare, and unopposed judges usually win.

Appointees to the six appellate courts and the supreme court also require the governor's nomination, but they must first be screened by the Commission on Judicial Nominees, a state agency whose members represent the legal profession, and then confirmed by the Commission on Judicial Appointments. Members of the latter include the attorney general, chief justice of the supreme court, presiding judge of the courts of appeal, and at-large members of the legal community who together evaluate appointees' fitness for office. Confirmation allows a justice to fulfill the remainder of his or her predecessor's twelve-year term, but the judge must participate in a nonpartisan "retention election" at the next gubernatorial election, at which time voters are asked to vote "yes" or "no" on whether a judge should remain in office. Judges may seek unlimited terms thereafter.

TABLE 6.1 Diversity of California's Justices and Judges

Court (persons reporting)	Female (N=523)	Male (N=1176)	Black or African American (N=95)	Hispanic or Latino (N=139)	Asian (N=92)	White (N=1229)	Native American/ Other/More than one (N=79)	Information not provided (N=59)
Supreme court (7)	57.1%	42.9%	0%	0%	28.6%	42.9%	28.6%	0%
Court of appeal (104)	32.7%	67.3%	4.8%	3.8%	2.9%	79.8%	6.7%	1.9%
Trial court (1,588)	30.6%	69.4%	5.7%	8.4%	5.5%	71.9%	4.2%	3.6%
Total	30.8%	69.2%	5.6%	8.2%	5.4%	72.3%	5.0%	3.5%

Source: Judicial Council of California, Administrative Office of the Courts, December 31, 2010, www.courts.ca.gov/2011 DemographicReport.pdf.

*In July 2011, Jerry Brown nominated UC Berkeley law professor Goodwin Liu to fill a vacancy on the supreme court. Liu is the only justice appointed by a Democratic governor.

Voters rarely reject judges. Defeat requires public outrage fed by a well-publicized, media-driven campaign, as three supreme court justices found in 1986. Having earned reputations for being "soft on crime" at a time when rising crime rates were rattling the public, Chief Justice Rose Bird and two of her colleagues were targeted for their opposition to the death penalty. For the first time in California history, three justices lost their retention bids, and Governor George Deukmejian replaced them with conservative justices.

Although judges rarely lose elections, they are not immune to campaign or interest group pressures. In the thirty-three states that directly elect judges, the price of judicial campaigns—even for retention elections—is rising, a trend that alarms court observers. Nationwide, several judicial elections in 2010 were targeted by "super spenders" and ideologically based interest groups hoping to sway the courts, a trend also apparent in smaller-scale contests.[7] In that election year for example, an outspoken Christian conservative group tried to unseat four superior court judges in San Diego by promoting its own candidates, sparking a larger debate over the integrity of California's court system. (All four judges managed to keep their jobs, despite relatively low turnout numbers.)

Judges can also be dismissed for improper conduct or incompetence arising from a range of activities, among them bias, inappropriate humor, and substance abuse. Hundreds of complaints are filed each year with the Commission on Judicial Performance, the independent state agency that investigates allegations of judicial misconduct. The commission does not review a justice's record but focuses instead on personal behavior that may warrant a warning letter, formal censure, removal, or forced retirement. Only a tiny fraction of judges face disciplinary action; the great majority have internalized the norms of judicial propriety that are imparted through law school and the legal community.

Court Administration

A supporting cast of thousands helps run the court system. The chief justice of the supreme court directs the operation from his or her position as chair of the thirty-one-member state Judicial Council of California, the public agency tasked with setting policy, rules, and procedures in accordance with ever-changing state law; making sure the court is accessible to citizens with diverse needs; and recommending improvements to the system. The council controls the judiciary's annual budget and reports to the legislature and responds to its mandates. With the help of administrative officers located at state courthouses, the council also manages the courts in a wide variety of ways; for instance, it makes information available to the public, keeps records, hires interpreters, schedules hearings, and assigns task forces to study issues such as foster care or domestic violence, among many other activities.

Juries

Barring a traffic violation, jury duty tends to be the average citizen's most direct link to the court system. Names of prospective jurors are randomly drawn from lists of registered voters and names provided by the Department of Motor Vehicles. Under the "one day-one trial" program, prospective jurors are excused from service at the end of the day if they have not been assigned to a trial, and they only need to respond to a summons once a year. If assigned to a trial, jurors consider questions of fact and weigh evidence to determine whether an accused person is guilty or not guilty. Convincing citizens to fulfill their duty isn't easy, and juries tend to over-represent those who have relatively more time on their hands, such as the elderly, the unemployed, and the wealthy. More than 9.4 million people serve on juries each year, though only one out of three people summoned to service actually sits on a trial.[8] All jurors are compensated $15 per day plus thirty-four cents for one-way mileage starting with the second day of service. There are no plans to raise this rate, though it is well below the national average of approximately $19 for the first day and $25 for the second day of service.[9]

Grand juries are impaneled every year in every county to investigate the conduct of city and county government and their agencies. Each contains nineteen members, except for Los Angeles's grand jury, which has twenty-three members due to the city's large population. During their one-year terms, grand jurors research claims of improper or wasteful practices, issue reports, recommend improvements to local programs, and sometimes indict political figures for misconduct, meaning they uncover sufficient evidence to warrant a trial.

Criminal Justice

About 90 percent of cases never make it to trial. High costs and delays associated with discovery, investigations, filings, and courtroom defense encourage out-of-court settlements and mediation, and the chance to receive a lesser sentence for pleading guilty results in plea bargains. Nevertheless, California's prisons are bursting at the seams for a number of reasons.

Topping the list of culprits is California's "three strikes" initiative. In 1994 voters were appalled at the abduction and murder of twelve-year-old Polly Klaas, a crime perpetrated by a man with a long and violent record. Klaas's family lobbied vigorously for tougher sentencing of repeat offenders, which culminated in the "three strikes and you're out" law: anyone convicted of a third felony is now sentenced to a mandatory twenty-five-years-to-life prison term without the possibility of parole, and penalties for second-strikers were also enhanced. Today, approximately forty-one thousand inmates are serving time for second and third strikes, most of which were nonviolent offenses.[10] Failure to build more prisons has also kept the prison population dangerously dense, and chronic underfunding has led to systemic deficiencies. In recent years the state has shifted over ten thousand convicted criminals through contracts with out-of-state facilities in states like Arizona, Mississippi, and Oklahoma. About 18,300 felons who are not legal residents also cost the state over $900 million per year because the federal government only reimburses less than 10 percent of the costs associated with their incarceration.

Prison populations have swelled under the three strikes and other mandatory sentencing laws, and so has spending on the approximately 163,000 inmates in facilities designed to hold about 85,000—by the Department of Corrections and Rehabilitation's admission, the state's prisons were 185 percent above capacity in early 2011.[11] In comparison, in 1980 the total prison population was 22,500, and in 1985 it cost less than $100 million to run the entire correctional system. At a yearly cost of $49,000 *per inmate,* spending on prisons and rehabilitation was just over $9 billion in 2009–2010. For each inmate approximately $16,000 is spent on mental, medical, and dental care; almost $34,000 goes to staff salary and benefits; and some of the remainder funds educational, vocational, and drug treatment programs.

Longer sentences translate into an aging prison population with escalating health issues, and prisoners are constitutionally guaranteed a right to medical care (the only group in the United States with this protected right), which is why a federal court put a federal official in control of regenerating the state's dysfunctional prison health care system when it was found to be unconstitutionally depriving inmates of their civil rights. Since that time the state has invested in upgrades, but federal courts have judged them insufficient and set deadlines to reduce the prison population, an unpleasant predicament for state decision makers accountable to citizens who think too much is spent on the corrections system. In fact, the only category of cuts that citizens consistently say they would support in order to balance the annual

BOX 6.1 FAST FACTS on California's Criminal Justice System

Enacted budget 2011–2012:	$9.85 billion
Cost per inmate:	$49,000
Staff:	64,932
Total number of inmates (estimated):	162,976*
Lifers:	24,579
Prisoners on death row:	697
Parolees:	107,879
Average sentence:	49 months
Average time served:	24.9 months
Number of prisons:	33, including minimum to maximum security; plus 39 camps, 13 community correctional facilities, and 5 prisoner mother facilities
Mean age (male and female):	38
Gender of inmates:	94% male, 6% female

Racial composition of inmate population:

Category	Inmate population
White, non-Hispanic	25.2%
Hispanic/Latino	39.8%
Black	28.9%
Other	6.1%

*Note: Due to reductions mandated by the federal government, this number is expected to decline further between 2011 and 2013.

Sources: Department of Corrections, "Prison Census Data as of Dec. 31, 2010," February 2011, www.cdcr.ca.gov/Reports_Research/Offender_Information_Services_Branch/Annual/Census/CENSUSd1012.pdf. Budget statistics from California Department of Finance, Governor's Budget 2011–2012, Enacted Budget Detail, http://www.ebudget.ca.gov/Enacted/StateAgencyBudgets/5210/5225/department.html.

budget is prisons and corrections: 62 percent supported this choice in May 2011.[12] Nevertheless state, prisoners will soon be released to satisfy a federal order to reduce overcrowding: about thirty-three thousand are slated for early release, transfer to county jails, or transfer to out of state institutions by 2013.

Crime rates have fallen in California over the past decade, and many point to the three strikes law as the reason. Crime rates and prison population trends in states that lack a three strikes law are similar to California's, however, and researchers have shown the cause-and-effect relationship to be complicated by other variables. Yet voters believe it works. They have been unwilling to soften sentencing laws that inflate state spending, as indicated by their rejection of a proposition in 2004 that would have restricted three-strikes sentencing to those who commit violent and serious offenses.

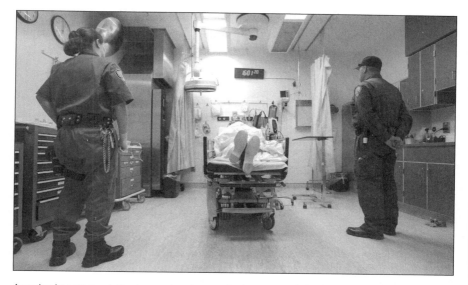

An aging inmate population has made prison medical care a costly business; the average annual cost per person is $16,000, with much higher price tags for specialized care—for example, it costs more than $800,000 a year to care for and guard a prisoner lying in a vegetative state. Under the Eighth Amendment's prohibition against cruel and unusual punishment, inmates are the only population in the United States guaranteed the constitutional right to receive adequate health care, although the quality of that care is often in doubt. Prompted by a class-action lawsuit in 2001 alleging dire conditions and the state's slowness to reform, a federal court removed control of prison health care from the state and appointed a federal receiver to help raise standards to an acceptable level and reduce costs. The receiver has remained in charge since 2005.

Conclusion: Administering Justice

As U.S. Supreme Court justice Anthony Kennedy noted, "The law commands allegiance only if it commands respect. It commands respect only if the public thinks the judges are neutral."[13] In their primary role as defenders of law and order, judges are expected to be independent arbiters of justice, and they must be particularly vigilant about respecting that ideal in California, where they are sometimes subject to politicizing cross-pressures applied through retention and recall election campaigns that are meant to hold them accountable. They play significant policymaking roles through the cases they choose at the appellate level and their interpretations of the law, defining the boundaries of acceptable behavior for businesses, government, and citizens. Judges are also subject to the impulses of voters through initiatives, just as other policymakers are. They help administer justice in a system that is sporadically reformed by propositions regarding sentencing of criminals, mandatory penalties, and even funding levels of the corrections system (indirectly thus far), and they must do so in a system that has experienced severe financial cutbacks.

Court proceedings offer concentrated insights into social ills such as poverty, lack of education, racism, unemployment, and homelessness that are manifest in crimes ranging from minor to serious. In California, judges are both leaders and partners in promoting law and order through the state's criminal justice system.

Notes

1. California Courts: The Judicial Branch of California, www.courtinfo.ca.gov.

2. Shane Goldmacher, "Chief Justice: 'Crippling' California Court Cuts Would Be 'a Blow against Justice,'" *Los Angeles Times*, June 14, 2011, http://latimesblogs.latimes.com/california-politics/2011/06/chief-justice-crippling-california-court-cuts-would-be-a-blow-against-justice-.html.

3. For those who can afford it, alternative dispute resolution (ADR), also known as mediation or legally binding arbitration, is a quicker way to decide cases. ADR relieves some pressure from the state's overall caseload, but it creates further divisions between those who can pay for high-priced mediators and those who must depend on state services.

4. Judicial Council of California, Administrative Office of the Courts, "2010 Court Statistics Report," http://www.courts.ca.gov/documents/csr2010.pdf

5. "George Deukmejian," *The Governors' Gallery*, http://governors.library.ca.gov/35-deuk mejian.html.

6. Julie Patel, "Forum Sheds Light on How Judges Are Screened, Chosen," *San Jose Mercury News*, June 4, 2006.

7. For more information about the politics and costs of judicial elections, see Justice at Stake Campaign, Brennan Center for Justice at NYU School of Law, "The New Politics of Judicial Elections: 2000-2009." www.justiceatstake.org/resources/new_politics_of_judicial_elections_20002009/.

8. Source: California Courts: The Judicial Branch of California, "About California Courts," September 2010, http://www.courts.ca.gov/2113.htm. Approximately 9.4 million persons completed service in 2008.

9. Based on data collected by The National Center for State Courts in 2007, the average compensation rate for the first day of service was $18.75 (plus mileage) and $25.30 for the second day (assuming juror was sworn in by day two). Data for some states was incomplete. See Gregory Mize, Paula Hannaford-Agor, and Nicole Waters, "The State of the States Survey of Jury Improvement Efforts: A Compendium Report," April 2007, www.ncsconline.org/D_Research/cjs/pdf/SOSCompendiumFinal.pdf.

10. Elizabeth Hill and Michael Genest, Letter to Edmund G. Brown, Attorney General (review of the proposed initiative cited as "The Three Strikes Reform Act of 2008"), November 29, 2007, www.lao.ca.gov/ballot/2007/070814.pdf.

11. Data Analysis Unit, Offender Information Services Branch, California Department of Corrections and Rehabilitation, May 3, 2011, http://www.cdcr.ca.gov/Reports_Research/Offender_Information_Services_Branch/Monthly/TPOP1A/TPOP1Ad1104.pdf.

12. Mark Baldassare et al, "Californians and their Government, May 2011," PPIC Statewide Survey, http://www.ppic.org/content/pubs/survey/S_511MBS.pdf.

13. Bill Moyers, "Justice for Sale: Interview with Justices Stephen Breyer and Anthony Kennedy," 1999, http://www.pbs.org/wgbh/pages/frontline/shows/justice/interviews/supremo.html.

Other Governments

Californians fall under the jurisdiction of many governments operating within the state's borders. Counties, cities, special districts, and regional governments share responsibility for delivering essential services that both protect and enhance residents' quality of life—from hiring police officers to making sure clean water flows beneath paved streets. Yet even in prosperous times these governments struggle to fund baseline operations with scarce taxpayer dollars. Demand for services outpaces voters' willingness to pay higher taxes for them.

The patchwork of subgovernments reflects historical demands for services along with the desire of communities for self-rule. In cases where one entity cannot or will not deliver a service, new ones have been created without regard to centralized planning. Bottom-up solutions are joined to state and federal mandates in a functionally segmented system— one that works with surprising efficiency for the number and scope of issues encompassed.

The revised state constitution of 1879 subdivided California into fifty-eight counties created to carry out programs created by the state government, and the boundaries have remained untouched since then. All but three of these counties (Alpine, Mariposa, and Trinity) contain cities within their boundaries. All counties contain large swaths of unincorporated areas where more than 20 percent of Californians reside and for which county governments directly provide services and local political representation. San Francisco is the only combination city/county.

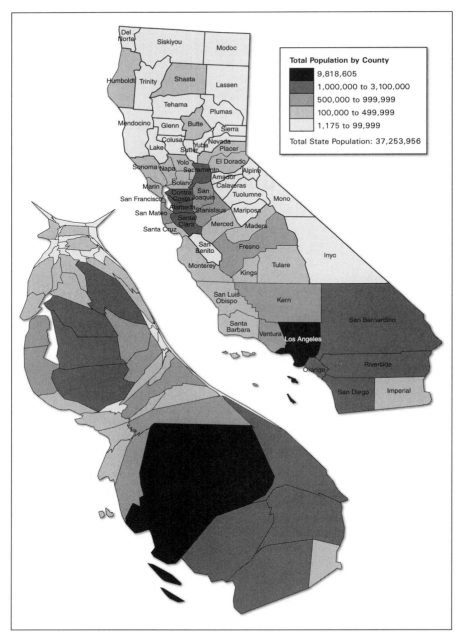

MAP 7.1

California, 2010 Population by County

Source: U.S. Census Bureau, 2010 Census, www.census.gov

Notes: Geographic area and population are two variables used to measure the size of California's fifty-eight counties. Geographic boundaries are shown in the top map with shadings for population density, and the lower "cartogram" illustrates the relative distribution of population by county. Small islands off of California's appear oversized because they are pictured as parts of respective counties. In actuality the islands are sparsely populated.

BOX 7.1 FAST FACTS on California's Other Governments

Number of counties:	58
Number of cities:	482
Special districts:	3,400
Five largest cities by population:	Los Angeles, 3,792,621
	San Diego, 1,307,402
	San Jose, 945,942
	San Francisco, 776,733
	Fresno, 494,665
Largest county by area:	San Bernardino, 20,052 square miles
Smallest county by area:	San Francisco, 47 square miles
	(10,000 people per sq. mi.)
Largest county by population:	Los Angeles, pop. 9,818,605
Smallest county by population:	Alpine, pop. 1,200
Smallest city:	Vernon, pop. 112
Number of chartered cities:	120 (24.9%)
Number of general law cities:	362 (75.1%)
Number of cities with directly elected mayors:	149 (30%)

Sources: U.S. Census Bureau 2010; California League of Cities.

County lines drawn in 1879 bear no relation to population density or economic activity today, and all counties are expected to provide the same kinds of services to their constituents regardless of population size or geographic area. This means that the largest county by population, Los Angeles, at more than 9.8 million, maintains the same baseline political departments, elected officials, and responsibilities as tiny Alpine, population twelve hundred.

Thirteen counties organize under **charters** that allow some flexibility in governing structure; forty-five others are organized according to state law. These forty-five **general law** counties are governed by five-member **boards of supervisors** (San Francisco's board has eleven members). Supervisors face nonpartisan elections every four years, and most are reelected overwhelmingly unless they are term-limited out after two, three, or four terms, and that depends on whether voters in a specific county have enacted such limits via local initiative. Many termed-out state lawmakers prolong their political careers as county supervisors, putting their knowledge and "institutional memory" about state issues and systems to good use by helping run the state's largest subgovernments.

Other elected county officials include the sheriff, district attorney, auditor/ controller, treasurer/tax collector, and clerk/recorder, all of whom help the board supply basic but vital social and political services in many areas:

PUBLIC SAFETY: courts, jails, probation, public defense, juvenile detention, sheriff, fire, emergency services

PUBLIC ASSISTANCE: housing, homeless, food stamps, state welfare programs

ELECTIONS & VOTING: voting processes, voter registration

TAX COLLECTION: county, city, special districts, schools

ENVIRONMENT & RECREATION: parks, facilities, open space, waste removal and recycling, air quality, land use, water

PUBLIC HEALTH: hospitals, mental health clinics, drug rehabilitation programs

EDUCATION: libraries, schools

SOCIAL SERVICES: adoptions, children's foster care

TRANSIT: airports, bus and rail systems, bridges, road maintenance

VITAL RECORDS: birth, death, marriage certificates

Counties finance these operations by levying sales taxes and user fees and through state government funds, property taxes, and federal grants, and they spend the most on public safety and public assistance (see Figures 7.1 and 7.2). State budget crises stem the flow of revenue, forcing counties to lay off employees, cut services, raise fees, or a combination of these measures to cover losses.

Municipal Government

Communities in unincorporated areas of a county may want more control over land use in their neighborhoods, better services, or a formal identity. They can petition their state-chartered local agency formation commission, or LAFCO, to incorporate as a city or municipality if their residents generate enough tax revenues to support a local government.

Much like counties, cities provide essential public services in the areas of public safety and emergency services; sewage and sanitation; public health; public works, including street maintenance; parks and recreation; libraries and schools; and land-use planning. Sometimes these overlap or supplement county programs: for example, a city might maintain its own library and also contain two or three county library branches. If lacking their own facilities, cities can contract with counties for services, pool their resources in a joint-powers agreement, or contract with private firms. A new trend among cities, especially as public employee pension obligations have grown over the years and residents have refused to pay higher taxes, has been to cut personnel and public works costs through outsourcing. One such "contract city" is the town of Half Moon Bay, which since 2011 has outsourced recreation services, engineering, legal services, code enforcement, and police protection, mostly to private contractors, the neighboring city of San Carlos, and San Mateo County.

More than 75 percent of California's 482 cities have incorporated under **general law,** meaning they follow state law in form and function. The remaining **charter cities** are creatures of local habits, formed through city constitutions that grant local government supreme authority over municipal affairs. This **"home rule" principle** permits municipal law to trump similar state laws. The City of Bell in the Los Angeles area serves as a severe reminder of this fact: using home rule to evade salary limitations that are set by state law, the city leaders of Bell voted themselves exorbitant pay raises that technically were legal. When finally exposed, the city manager was making almost $800,000 a year in salary and benefits—more than four times the governor's salary!

Virtually every city is governed by a five-member **city council** that concentrates on passing and implementing local laws, called **ordinances**. Thus, unlike how state and federal governments separate powers among different branches to ensure checks and balances, legislating *and* executing local law blends in city councils. City councils rely heavily on small boards and **commissions** filled by local volunteers or appointees to help recommend and set policy relating to the special needs of citizens and businesses. For example, the City of Gardena has seven commissions, one of which is the Youth Commission, responsible for identifying and evaluating community programs, problems, and concerns relating to youths. There is also a Senior Citizens Commission. To facilitate public participation in these and other public-planning bodies, as at the state level, all city and county governing institutions must abide by the **Brown Act**, which mandates advance notice of meetings, "open meetings," and full public disclosure of proceedings.

City council members are reelected every four years in nonpartisan elections, usually by the entire city's electorate in an **at-large election** rather than from separate **districts**. Many city councils are now subject to local voter-imposed term limits, and the list of term-limited cities grows each year. If the **mayor** is not elected at-large (meaning that the whole city votes for mayor), council members designate one among them to act as a ceremonial mayor, typically on a rotating basis, for one or two years at a time. Each city makes its own rules regarding how long and how often city council members can act as mayor and whether the appointment will be automatic, by acclamation, or by election. Automatic rotation creates opportunities for many young council members to assume the role of mayor, and mayors in their twenties are not altogether uncommon. Ceremonial mayors lack veto power, and their vote on the council is equal to that of their colleagues.

If the mayor's authority exceeds that of the city council members, such as the power to veto city council actions or hire and fire high-profile appointees to help run city operations, a **strong mayor** form of government is in place. Some 30 percent of California cities maintain this form of municipal government, partly because a sole individual can offer a clear agenda and be held accountable for its success or failure. The far more popular **council-manager system** exists in nearly 70 percent of cities, an institutional legacy of Progressives who believed that efficient city management required technical expertise because "there is no partisan way to pave a street." In most cities then, a council retains a ceremonial mayor but hires a

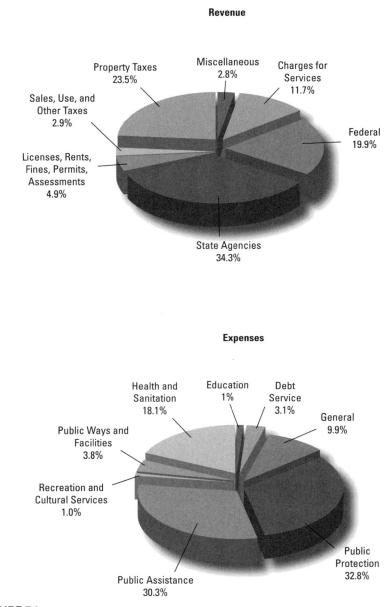

Revenue

Property Taxes
23.5%

Miscellaneous
2.8%

Charges for
Services
11.7%

Sales, Use, and
Other Taxes
2.9%

Federal
19.9%

Licenses, Rents,
Fines, Permits,
Assessments
4.9%

State Agencies
34.3%

Expenses

Health and
Sanitation
18.1%

Education
1%

Debt
Service
3.1%

General
9.9%

Public Ways and
Facilities
3.8%

Recreation and
Cultural Services
1.0%

Public
Protection
32.8%

Public Assistance
30.3%

FIGURE 7.1

County Revenues and Expenses, 2008–2009

Source: California State Controller, "Counties Annual Report," prepared June 30, 2010.

Note: Excludes the city/county of San Francisco.

City councils make laws (their legislative function includes passing ordinances) and also execute laws by implementing city plans or programs. The San Bernardino City Council regularly meets twice weekly, compared to Los Angeles's city council, which meets three times a week, or the councils of smaller cities that commonly meet twice a month. At a typical meeting council members might discuss pending litigation, decide land use matters, pay tribute to community heroes, approve expenses and payments for city services, establish new fees, expend grant revenue, set salaries for city employees or eliminate positions, set contracts for city services, and/or address citizens' concerns on a range of issues.

professional **city manager** to budget for, manage, and oversee the day-to-day operations of a city. As a city's "chief executive officer," the city manager is authorized to make decisions independent of the council and thus wields great power behind the scenes. The office handles hiring and firing decisions, as well as the supervision of all city departments. Most city managers possess a master's degree in public administration and have experience managing local government departments.

Cities depend heavily on taxes and fees to finance operations. Prior to Proposition 13, property taxes constituted 57 percent of combined city and county revenues annually; in 2008–2009 property taxes represented only 8.4 percent of the average aggregate city budget. The bulk of funding now comes from sales and use taxes; fines and developer fees; service charges for public utilities and transit; a variety of taxes on hotels, other businesses, and property; and state and federal agencies.

Assembly members and senators perform economic gymnastics to balance the state budget during hard times, and their routine includes yanking property taxes and other fees previously committed to cities to "backfill" the state's budget hole. In an effort to stop such state "raiding" of local funds, cities and counties sponsored a

Revenue

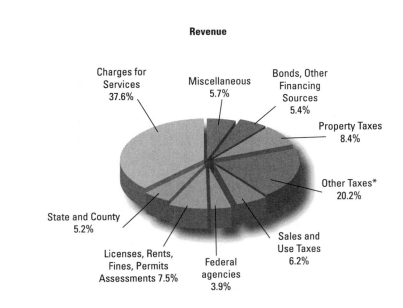

Charges for
Services
37.6%

Miscellaneous
5.7%

Bonds, Other
Financing
Sources
5.4%

Property Taxes
8.4%

Other Taxes*
20.2%

State and County
5.2%

Sales and
Use Taxes
6.2%

Licenses, Rents,
Fines, Permits
Assessments 7.5%

Federal
agencies
3.9%

*Includes transportation, transient lodging, franchises, business license, real property transfer, utility users, and other nonproperty taxes. Excludes San Francisco.

Expenses

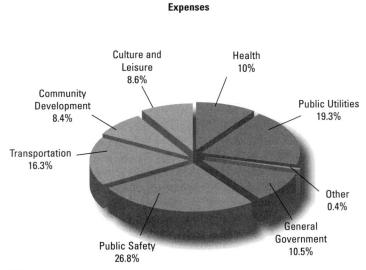

Culture and
Leisure
8.6%

Health
10%

Community
Development
8.4%

Public Utilities
19.3%

Transportation
16.3%

Other
0.4%

General
Government
10.5%

Public Safety
26.8%

FIGURE 7.2

City Revenues and Expenses, 2008–2009

Source: State Controller's Office, Cities Annual Report prepared June 30, 2010.

Note: Excludes the city/county of San Francisco.

constitutional amendment to prevent the state from transferring locally generated property taxes, vehicle license fees, and sales taxes into the state's general fund. Though voters approved Proposition 1A in 2004, the state has overridden some of those restrictions during fiscal crises, as it did for the 2009–2010 budget. Facing losses amounting to millions of dollars, cities (and counties) scramble to find substitute revenue sources. One popular strategy at the city level is to charge developers heavy fees for new construction projects or saddle them with the costs of constructing new streets, schools, sewers, or any infrastructure improvements related to population growth.

Another strategy is to base land-use decisions on a project's net fiscal impact, a phenomenon known as the **fiscalization of land use.** In practical terms this means that cities today have incentives to entice and keep retail businesses that can generate substantial sales taxes, as local governments receive 1 percent of state sales taxes collected in their jurisdictions. Auto dealerships, shopping malls, and big-box retailers like Wal-Mart are therefore favored over low-income housing and service-based industries that will further stress city resources—in other words, decisions are made without regard to the intrinsic value of, or need for, a project.

For several decades, **redevelopment districts** have also brought some measure of relief. Ranging from one to 85,000 acres, these districts are created by designating economically distressed or "blighted" areas for revitalization; neglected buildings are torn down, refuse is cleared away, and new infrastructure and facilities such as affordable housing or community centers are built. Property taxes are artificially capped within those zones, and cities are entitled to keep the additional property taxes that are paid after properties are improved—an overall value that Governor Brown's office estimated at 12 percent of all property taxes, representing $5 billion in annual property tax revenue.[1] Approximately 80 percent of cities contain a redevelopment agency, or RDA, that oversees ongoing redevelopment activities. To help balance the budget in 2011, Governor Brown proposed dissolving all four hundred RDAs with the intent to return all excess tax benefits to the state (ostensibly to be used for funding schools, police and fire protection, and other districts), citing improperly invested funds and the state's budgetary needs. Advocates for cities and RDAs with ongoing projects have sued the state over this plan, which was incorporated in the 2011 budget, and the state supreme court was set to decide by January 2012 whether the plan could be implemented.

Special Districts

Special districts are geographic areas governed by an autonomous board for a single purpose, such as running an airport or providing communities with street lighting or cemeteries. Arguably the most abundant power centers in California but virtually invisible to the average citizen, special districts proliferate because they are created to meet critical needs that cities and counties lack the will or capacity to address. Like regular governments, they can sue and be sued, charge users for their services, and exercise the right to eminent domain (the taking of property for public use). Unlike most governments however, their domains may cover only a portion of a city or stretch across several cities or counties.

Clothing, cars, televisions, and many other goods pass through this important special district, the Port of Los Angeles at San Pedro, before being transported to stores across the United States. Located twenty miles from downtown Los Angeles, the port occupies forty-three miles of waterfront and handles 190 million metric revenue tons of cargo annually, making it the busiest cargo port in the nation. Ports are major economic engines, sustaining hundreds of thousands of jobs. If combined with neighboring Long Beach port, the area would be the sixth-largest port in the world, following those in Asia. The Port of Long Beach alone generates about $14.5 billion in annual trade-related wages.

Of 4,700 special districts in the state, two-thirds operate independently with their own boards of governors chosen by voters in low-profile elections; the remainder are controlled by counties or cities through appointments. About 2,700 special districts independently generate their own revenue as enterprises through fees or for providing services and charging their customers, while the remainder depend on counties and cities for their funding. The majority of special district services are paid for through property-related service charges or special assessments that initially require a two-thirds majority vote. In other words, the total fee per property owner will be a percentage of a property's assessed value, so neighbors might pay different rates for the same services. The Southern California Metropolitan Water District (MWD) epitomizes this fee-based service: created by the legislature in 1928, its mission is to provide adequate, reliable supplies of high-quality drinking water to current and future residents in southern California. Today, twenty-six cities and water districts coordinate their activities through the MWD to provide drinking water to nineteen million residents in six counties, delivering over 1.9 billion gallons of water daily. In addition to paying their local water district for the water they use, Southern California residents see charges listed on their annual property tax bill for basic MWD services.

School districts comprise a separate but most familiar category of special district: more than 1,000 provide K–12 education for about 6.2 million students attending almost 10,000 different schools; an additional seventy-two districts encompass 112 community colleges.[2] Created by state law, nonpartisan five-member boards of education (Los Angeles's board has seven) govern their school districts by following the detailed operating instructions of the state's education code and heeding the State Board of Education's mandates. An appointed superintendent manages the local system, which may be responsible for almost 700,000 students—as is the case in the gargantuan Los Angeles system—or fewer than twenty students, which is the case in twenty-three districts (although the nonpartisan California Legislative Analyst's Office has recommended that the state increase the minimum size for all school districts to at least one hundred students). Governing boards handle issues relating to nearly every aspect of student life, from regulating students' cell phone use to defining nutritional needs to designing appropriate curricula, and they must consider the vocal parents and special interest groups trying to influence their decisions.

Proposition 98 dedicates approximately 40 percent of the state's general fund budget to K–14 education, yet based on the 2009-2010 budget, this translates into only 56 percent of the money that schools receive. The rest comes from a variety of sources: approximately 14.5 percent of education funds are federal dollars, 19.5 percent comes from property taxes that were previously directed to cities, and miscellaneous sources supply the remaining 10.5 percent, including special local parcel taxes or private donations.

A Contra Costa County Mosquito and Vector Control District technician prepares to treat a mosquito-infested pool at a foreclosed home in Concord, California. Vector control districts protect public health by containing the spread of diseases such as malaria and West Nile Virus that are borne by mosquitoes.

Regional Governments

Regional governments plan, regulate, and coordinate land-use and development-related activities across counties and cities by providing a permanent forum in which local leaders can discuss ideas and exchange information. State law vests regional governments with authority for housing and transportation planning, but, more broadly, **councils of government** (COGs) plan for future populations by addressing issues that transcend boundaries and encompass a wide spectrum of common infrastructure-related needs, including food and water availability, public safety, and environmental quality. There are twenty-five major COGs in California, plus six sub-COGs in the Southern California Association of Governments, or SCAG.

COGs coordinate rather than dictate because they cannot force decisions on local governments. Their governing boards are composed of mayors, city council members, and county supervisors, and they receive input from research specialists and advisers from federal departments, special districts, state agencies, and even Mexico. Their planning activities include reviewing federal grants-in-aid and proposing legislation. They do not deliver public services.

Regional government may also take the form of regulatory entities that set rules for environmentally sensitive activities. For instance, California's thirty-five "air districts" are dedicated to controlling pollution from stationary sources (Air Pollution Control Districts, or APCDs) and promoting air quality (Air Quality Management Districts, or AQMDs) through comprehensive planning programs that include the setting of compulsory rules for residents and the enforcement of those rules, air quality monitoring, research, public education, and the issuing of special business permits.

Federalism

Whereas the state authorizes county governments, local jurisdictions, and special districts to perform necessary functions, the U.S. Constitution guarantees that states share governing power with the national government, although states' authority has diminished as both the federal purse and federal capacity have grown. The U.S. Congress discovered long ago that **funding** is a convenient instrument for enticing states to adopt federal goals by granting or withholding monies in exchange for new state policy. In this way, highway funds have been exchanged for lower speed limits and setting the drinking age at twenty-one—issues that only the states can legislate.

California is also subject to **unfunded mandates**. These are federal laws that require the states to provide services, but no federal funds are supplied to implement them. Such mandates amount to hundreds of millions of dollars in such areas as social services, transportation, education, health care, and cleaning up

BOX 7.2 The Feds vs. California on Air Quality

In protest of the federal government's neglect of climate change for far too long, in an unprecedented move the state's majority-Democratic legislature joined Governor Arnold Schwarzenegger in crafting the Global Warming Solutions Act of 2006, otherwise known as Assembly Bill 32 (AB 32), the world's first law establishing a program of regulatory and market mechanisms to curb emissions of greenhouse gases. Though businesses and anti-regulatory interests continue to strongly oppose the law, anticipating higher costs because of its mandates, voters beat back an initiative (Proposition 23) to rescind it in 2010. Importantly, the new law authorizes the state's Air Resources Board to:

1. set a statewide emissions cap for 2020, based on 1990 emissions levels;
2. adopt mandatory reporting rules for significant sources of greenhouse gases;
3. establish advisory boards to assist with planning; and
4. advance a plan indicating how much emissions reduction will be achieved through regulations, market mechanisms, and other actions. Two of the major steps of the new plan are:
    a. A state-administered cap-and-trade program. This market-based system sets an overall limit on greenhouse gas (GHG) emissions, and facilities that emit GHG will be granted a certain amount of allowances to emit those gases. Companies that emit less than their allowance will be able to sell or trade their credits to companies that exceed their allowances
    b. The setting of fuel efficiency standards for new cars, trucks, and sport utility vehicles sold in California by 2012

Initially the act was fiercely opposed by a tight coalition of automobile, manufacturing, and energy industries, which challenged the new law as going "too far" by setting stricter standards than the federal government—despite the fact that the Environmental Protection Agency (EPA) had never set a greenhouse gas emissions standard. Ruling that AB 32 superseded federal authority to maintain clean air standards, the EPA under the George W. Bush administration denied California a waiver from adhering to lower national clean air standards set in the Federal Clean Air Act. On June 30, 2009, the EPA under the Barack Obama administration reversed the ruling, giving California the "green light" to proceed with implementation and enforcement of AB 32. "This decision puts the law and science first,"* stated EPA administrator Lisa Jackson when announcing the decision, which also affects the District of Columbia and the thirteen other states that have followed California's lead. Schwarzenegger issued his own statement: "After being asleep at the wheel for over two decades, the federal government has finally stepped up and granted California its nation-leading tailpipe emissions waiver....California's long battle to reduce pollution from passenger vehicles is over, and a greener, cleaner future has finally arrived."**

Source: California Air Resources Board.

*Environmental Protection Agency, "EPA Grants California GHG Waiver," June 30, 2009, http://yosemite.epa.gov/opa/admpress.nsf/bd4379a92ceceeac8525735900400c27/5e448236de5fb369852575e500568e1b!OpenDocument.

**California Governor's Office, "Governor Applauds EPA Decision Granting California Authority to Reduce Greenhouse Gas Emissions," June 30, 2009, http://gov.ca.gov/issue/energy-environment.

the environment. For example, a recent Government Accountability Office report found that housing undocumented immigrants in state correctional facilities cost the state about $34,000 per inmate, or $1.1 billion in 2009.[3] Mandates also can take the form of **preemptive legislation,** which prohibits a state from passing certain laws; this has been done to prevent some of California's progressive environmental rules and legislation from taking effect, such as a ban on ride-on lawn mowers—a move that would negatively impact the states where they are manufactured.

California remains dependent on the federal government to balance its ledgers, receiving billions for major programs such as welfare and health coverage—all told, a figure approaching $80 *billion* for the 2011–2012 fiscal year, or 38 percent of total state spending, which is close to $209 billion. Yet imbalances persist. Californians tend to pay more in federal taxes than they receive overall: outside of federal stimulus payments of the kind made in 2009–2010, one source estimates that Californians normally receive about seventy-eight cents for every dollar paid in taxes.[4] When he took office, former governor Schwarzenegger swore to become "The Collectinator" by convincing Washington to send home the billions that Californians overpay annually,[5] but he was remarkably unsuccessful despite the activity of fifty-three U.S. representatives and two powerful U.S. senators, the ascension of Californian Nancy Pelosi as Speaker of the House from 2006–2010, and the appointment of Californians to chair powerful federal congressional committees—leadership positions through which federal dollars could be funneled back to the state. The imbalance can be blamed partly on the fact that California is a wealthy state and federal taxes are progressive, meaning that Californians (just as citizens in other high-income states like Connecticut) simply send more to Washington. This, combined with factors such as a decrease in military bases in the state and a younger population, means that fewer Californians receive checks from the government (Medicare, Social Security) than in states with a lower income rate per capita (Alabama, Mississippi).

Tribal Governments

Tribal governments operated in relative obscurity until recently. Isolated on one hundred thousand acres of remote and frequently inhospitable reservations throughout California, the state's 108 tribes had minimal impact on neighboring cities or state government. Native groups were defined politically by their interaction with the U.S. Congress and federal agencies, as well as by prior case law that treated them as wards of the federal government rather than as fully sovereign nations. In the main, California governments could ignore them.

Gaming changed all that. As bingo halls flourished in the 1970s and blossomed into full-scale gambling enterprises by the late 1980s, states began looking for ways to limit, eliminate, tax, influence, or otherwise control this new growth industry, one whose environmental and social effects on surrounding communities were proving significant.

After the U.S. Supreme Court ruled in 1987 that tribes do indeed have the right to run gambling enterprises on their lands, Congress exercised its supreme lawmaking authority (to which tribes are subject) and wrote the **Indian Gaming Regulatory Act (IGRA),** a law that restricts the scope of gaming and defers regulatory authority to the states. The IGRA also stipulates that tribes within a state and the state itself must enter into compacts to permit certain forms of gaming irrespective of tribal sovereignty.

No state can collect taxes from tribal nations, but California governor Gray Davis used this point as a bargaining chip with sixty-one tribes during their compact negotiations in the late 1990s. The final compact specified that in exchange for permitting Las Vegas–style gambling, tribes would participate in revenue-sharing with nongaming tribes and also contribute to a fund for reimbursing casino-related costs to cities and counties, such as those related to traffic congestion, public safety, and gambling addiction. California voters overwhelmingly approved this first compact as Proposition 5, which was superseded two years later by constitutional amendment Proposition 1A in 2000. Gaming compacts that are renegotiated over time eventually take the form of referendums submitted to voters for approval. This recently occurred when several Southern California tribes negotiated a deal to add thousands of slot machines in exchange for millions more paid annually into the state's general fund. Native American groups spent a combined $108.4 million to convince voters to approve four propositions in 2008, and each passed by at least 55.5 percent.[6] Today, the state's casino industry is exceeded in size only by that of Nevada, and more than half of the state's slot machines are located in three Southern California counties: San Diego, Riverside, and San Bernardino. Eleven Native American casinos were expanded or renovated in 2009, bringing the total number of gaming machines to over sixty-six thousand.

The U.S. Constitution explicitly recognizes four sovereigns:

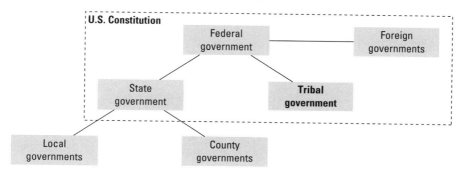

FIGURE 7.3

Tribes Are Recognized Sovereigns

Source: Kate Spilde, Kenneth Grant and Jonathan Taylor, "Commentary: Social and Economic Consequences of Indian Gaming in Oklahoma," *American Indian Culture and Research Journal* 28, no. 2 (Los Angeles: UCLA American Indian Studies Center, 2004). Reprinted with permission of the authors.

Clearly, "tribal sovereignty" has limits with regard to both federal and state law. Tribes retain control over political activities within their reservation's borders, and their governments usually take the form of all-powerful tribal councils vested with executive, legislative, and judicial powers. Councils have full control over tribal membership, which numbers more than fifty thousand registered individuals in California alone, and they implement federal assistance and grants covering health care, education, and other social needs, which amounts to about $278 million in direct payments and grants per year.[7]

Gaming operations have laid the foundation for socioeconomic and political development in and around tribal territories. Relative prosperity has transformed tribal governments into fully staffed operations that have increasing institutional capacity to provide services that the state can't or won't provide. Tribes are now important participants in regional planning, and cities, counties, and local communities benefit from their charitable donations, jobs, and tax revenues. Additionally, the state benefits from their ability to obtain federal dollars for improvement projects, such as widening roads and building bridges in cases where such upgrades are otherwise unaffordable. California tribes make themselves indispensible to the state government by making annual payments to the general fund. They paid approximately $364 million out of a total estimated $6.95 billion in casino revenues

The Morongo Casino Resort and Spa rises above the desert floor near the San Jacinto Mountains. The Morongo Band of Mission Indians in Cabazon, California, operates one of fifty-eight tribal gaming enterprises in the state; California has ratified compacts with 67 tribes. The fact that casinos must be located on existing tribal lands naturally limits their expansion. Gaming revenues have helped reduce the percentage of Native American families living in poverty, which remained high in 2009 at 26 percent.

in 2009, but these figures have dropped significantly with the economic downturn and are not expected to increase in the next few years.[8]

Gaming enterprises have transformed tribal governments into major players at both the state and national levels, enabling them to lobby for or against policies of interest to them and donate heavily to campaigns. Tribes nationwide contributed approximately $10.4 million to political campaigns in the 2008 cycle, favoring Democrats by 75 percent.[9] The industry spent nearly $17.8 million on federal lobbying during the following year, though their overall spending has decreased from a high in 2004.

Conclusion: The State's Interlocking Systems

California's state government is much more than a mega-institution with a few major components. Instead, the state's government should be viewed as a complex organism, with approximately 5,700 identifiable working parts found in counties, cities, special districts, and regions, in addition to the state's courts, administration, and legislature. Each part contributes to the welfare of the whole, either singly or in conjunction with others, but never in isolation. When dissected, the system appears as a bewildering mess of overlapping boundary lines, yet these interlocking systems provide essential services that citizens need and will continue to demand.

Notes

1. Costs estimated for 2011–2012. Source: Department of Finance, "Redevelopment Agency Dissolution and Succession," draft proposal, February 23, 2011, http://www.dof .ca.gov/budgeting/trailer_bill_language/financial_research_and_local_government/ documents/502%20RDA%20Legislation%202-23p.pdf.

2. Statistics are for the 2009–2010 school year, published by the state's Department of Education on their data Web site, Ed-Data.k-12.ca.us (see state reports). See also the 2010 *Fact Book*, www.cde.ca.gov/re/pn/fb.

3. California housed more than 102,795 criminal aliens in 2009. Costs reported in 2010 dollars by the U.S. Government Accountability Office, "Criminal Alien Statistics: Information of Incarcerations, Arrests, and Costs, (GAO-11-187)." March 2011 (p. 40). www.gao.gov/new .items/d11187.pdf.

4. This number is based on somewhat dated figures (2005) from the U.S. Tax Foundation. There is some dispute over how to accurately calculate these figures; much depends on which taxes and which federal expenditures are considered. See "Federal Taxes Paid vs. Federal Spending Received by State, 1981–2005," October 19, 2007, http://www.taxfoundation.org/ taxdata/show/22685.html.

5. Data compiled from the California Institute for Federal Policy Research, "California's Balance of Payments with the Federal Treasury, 1981–2004," www.calinst.org/index.html.

6. Vote results supplied by California Secretary of State. Data taken from follow themoney.org, Ballot measure summaries for Propositions 94–97", www.followthemoney .org/database/StateGlance/ballot.phtml?m=493.

7. Data taken from the U.S. Census Bureau, *Consolidated Federal Funds Report 2009*, http://harvester.census.gov/cffr/asp/Geography.asp.

8. Data taken from the 2011–2012 Governor's Budget Summary, January 10, 2011, http://www.ebudget.ca.gov/pdf/BudgetSummary/FullBudgetSummary.pdf. The National Indian Gaming Commission reported that total revenues for forty-nine gaming operations in California and northern Nevada tribes was $6,969,881 in FY 2008 and $7,363,493 for fifty-nine operations in FY 2008. Source: http://www.nigc.gov/linkclick.aspx?fileticket=goZCPYP DuT4%3d&tabid=67.

9. Data taken from Opensecrets.org, "Indian Gaming: Background," November 2010, www.opensecrets.org/industries/background.php?cycle=2010&ind=G6550.

CHAPTER 8

The California Budget Process

> "The best evidence of the fairness of any settlement is the fact that
> it fully satisfies neither party."
>
> –Winston Churchill, 1926

Annual budgeting at the state level is a grueling process of translating social and political values into dollars, made all the more punishing by uncontrollable economic crises that make dollars disappear. A budget is also a statement of priorities, the result of intense bargaining, and the product of a sophisticated guessing game about future income and spending that provides risk-averse politicians with incentives to use accounting tricks to make things look rosier than they really are. But gargantuan deficits can't be papered over, and as California's government floundered while the economic emergency grew during the 2000s, the state's ungovernability continued to make national headlines as constitutional closing dates came and went, and falling revenues made balancing the books even harder.

Why can't lawmakers and governors effectively solve the state's budget problems, especially during economic crises when their solutions are most needed? "Why," many Californians ask, "do we pay so much in taxes, but the state never has enough?" This chapter examines the budgeting process and explores the reasons for California's budgetary dilemmas—dilemmas that force representatives to make painful choices among alternatives.

California Budgeting 101

California's fiscal year (FY) begins July 1 and ends June 30. By law a new budget must be passed by June 15 or lawmakers forfeit their pay (a new condition imposed by voters in 2010); it must then be signed by July 1 or the state cannot pay for services that it hasn't yet authorized for the new cycle. In past years the budget was routinely completed late, triggering more uncertainty and panic for Californians dependent on state services, but the on-time budget in 2011 indicates that losing their own paycheck provides lawmakers with strong incentives to be punctual. Excluding delays, it takes at least eighteen months to construct the state's spending plan.

Advance work begins in the governor's **Department of Finance (DOF)**, which is staffed by professional analysts who continuously collect data about state operations. Each branch of government and executive department itemizes its own programmatic budget needs, from personnel to project costs, including items such as habitat restoration (Department of Fish and Game), managed care for people with disabilities (Health and Human Services), and trial court funding (judicial branch)—merely a sampling from among thousands of state government activities. The DOF's projections about how much money will be available through taxes and fees provide baselines for estimating how much *must* be spent on major existing programs and how much *can* be spent on new desired programs or services. **Mandatory spending** absorbs most of the approximately $85–$100 billion annual budgets, leaving limited room for legislators to duke it out for the **discretionary** funds used to cover all other state services, from monitoring the safety of amusement rides to sheltering victims of domestic violence.

Guided by the governor's initiatives, political values, and stated objectives, the DOF prepares a budget by assigning dollar amounts to state programs and services. The governor submits his budget to the legislature by January 10, whereupon it is routed to the legislature's own **legislative analyst** for scrutiny. Heeding recommendations from the Legislative Analyst's Office (LAO) and anticipating the governor's updated version that takes into account actual tax receipts (the **May Revision or "May Revise"**), throughout the spring the legislative budget committees and subcommittees work on the legislature's own competing version of the budget. State analysts testify before the committees, as do officials, lobbyists, and citizens representing every sector of society and government as they seek protection for existing benefits or beg for more.

Once the budget committees finalize their work and the legislature resolves its differences into a comprehensive budget bill (usually through the help of a conference committee comprised of three members from each house), legislative leaders and their staffs begin negotiating with the governor and his or her staff to reach compromises. Will money be set aside for emergency spending in a "rainy day" fund? If so, will that money come from cuts to mental health programs or afterschool care? How much of a "hit" will the college and university systems bear? Will domestic violence shelters be closed? Hundreds of decisions like these play into negotiations that routinely used to include the party leaders from both houses (along with the governor, they constitute the "**Big Five**") until the primary responsibility for passing the budget was shifted to the majority party (according to Proposition 25 in 2010, a simple majority is sufficient to pass it). As was the case following the 2010 elections, when the same party controls the governorship and both legislative chambers, minority party leaders will ultimately be excluded from the top-level negotiations if they refuse to compromise on issues the majority party considers fundamental, and if the minority's votes are not ultimately necessary for passing the budget. Thus, the "**Big Three**" (the governor, the Speaker, and the president pro tem, all Democrats) were the key players in 2011.

Final agreements also hinge on the governor's line-item veto power (see chapter 5). Eventually, often after considerable debate and struggle, the budget is passed and signed into law, as are "**trailer bills**"—a package of omnibus or large bills that make the necessary policy changes to the state laws and codes outlined in the budget plan.

After vetoing the first budget bill sent to his desk, Governor Jerry Brown signed the annual state budget into law on June 30, 2011 with Speaker John Pérez and President Pro Tem Darrell Steinberg of the senate flanking him. Ultimately, the "Big Three" negotiated the FY 2011–12 budget without the cooperation of Republican leaders, and their plan was the first on-time budget in five years, probably due in part to a new law stating that legislators would lose their pay every day the budget was late.

Mechanics of Budgeting: Revenue

A budget reflects the governor's and legislature's educated guesses about how much money the state will collect in taxes, fees, and federal grants during the coming year, as well as the state's commitments to spending or saving what it collects. All budgets are built on economic data, assumptions, and formulas designed to produce accurate forecasts about dollar amounts and the numbers of people who will demand the services and products these dollar amounts pay for. Relatively small numerical shifts can equal hundreds of millions of dollars. For instance, the state controller reported that in June 2009 the state's three largest sources of revenue were 0.6 percent—just a bit more than *half of a percentage point*—below what had been predicted a month earlier in the May Revision, a difference equaling *$499 million*. Projections can occasionally work the other way too: Governor Jerry Brown's 2011 May Revision reflected tax revenues that were over $6 billion higher than what was anticipated just three months prior. Larger economic forces produce discrepancies like these that cannot be estimated precisely. Nevertheless, sophisticated assumptions about how much will be coming into the state's coffers serve as a foundation for balancing the budget—or at least making it *appear* balanced.

Revenue is another word for income. The largest revenue streams are provided by **taxes** and **fees** for services, and in 2010–2011 these helped raise the state's general fund revenues to $94 billion, or $120 billion in total state income if special funds and bonds are taken into account. Taxes are deposited into the state's general fund or redistributed to county and local governments; special fuel taxes go into the transportation fund. It should be noted that property taxes are raised at the local level and mainly used to fund schools; they do not augment the general fund. **Bond** funds are borrowed funds that are designated for specific purposes. In 2010–2011 bonds contributed $8 billion to the total state budget.

A separate stream of revenue, **federal grant money**, is funneled through the federal fund, representing billions of dollars from the United States government that go straight to state and local governments to subsidize specific programs such as Medi-Cal or local entities for a variety of services such as low-income housing or school lunches. The Department of Finance estimated federal transfers were $92 billion in FY 2010–2011, a figure augmented by short-lived federal stimulus funds. When considering these federal dollars, the entire state budget for FY 2011–2012 will actually exceed $208 billion.

The state relies on several major categories of taxes, all of which are highly sensitive to larger economic trends. In other words, taxes rise and fall with the economy, creating unpredictable swings in tax collection. **Personal income taxes** contribute the greatest portion of state revenues nationwide; in California it is indeed the most important source, totaling almost $50 billion in FY 2010–2011, more than *half* of the state's general fund revenue. (The figure is closer to 40 percent of the *total* budget, which includes revenue from all state sources, meaning all taxes, special funds, and bonds). California's personal income taxes are progressive, meaning that tax rates increase along with income so that people at the higher end of the income scale are charged a greater percentage in taxes than those at the lower end. Current

TABLE 8.1 General Obligation Bonds Passed, 2006–2008

2006	Bond	Cost	Purpose
Transportation	Proposition 1B	$19,900,000,000	Maintaining and expanding highways and roads, ports, passenger rail systems; bridge retrofitting
Natural resources	Proposition 84	$5,400,000,000	Water system planning; flood control; beach, bays, parks, and waterway protection
Education	Proposition 1D	$10,400,000,000	$7.3 billion for modernizing and expanding K–12 schools; $3.1 billion to the University of California, California State University, and community colleges
Natural resources	Proposition 1E	$4,100,000,000	Flood control
2008			
Transportation	Proposition 1A	$9,900,000,000	High-speed rail system
Children's hospitals	Proposition 3	$900,000,000	Constructing and improving children's hospitals
Veterans' Bond Act	Proposition 12	$900,000,000	Veterans' home loan program
TOTAL 2006–2008		**$51,500,000,000**	

Source: Adapted from Dean Misczynski, "Just the Facts: California's Debt," February 2009, Public Policy Institute of California, www.ppic.org/content/pubs/jtf/JTF_CADebtJTF.pdf.

rates range from 1 to 10.3 percent (the top bracket applies to those making more than $1 million per year, what some call "soaking the rich"), though taxpayers can receive various exemptions and credits to offset the total they owe.

Retail sales and use taxes are the second-largest source of California's income, accounting for almost a third of the state's general fund revenue (about 25 percent of the total budget). Sales generated $31 billion in taxes in FY 2010–2011, an amount based on the base state sales tax rate that the legislature temporarily raised by one cent (to 8.25 percent) to help close the budget gap. If legislators or voters neither extend nor raise the **base rate of 7.25 percent** in 2012, then 5.25 percent goes to the general fund and 2 percent is re-allocated to local governments. Consumer spending directly affects how much money is available to cover state expenses, and spending patterns during economic recessions have resulted in multibillion-dollar losses to state governments. This also applies to excise taxes for goods such as fuel, the demand for which tends to decline as unemployment rates and fuel costs rise.

Corporate income taxes represent a much smaller piece of the revenue pie ($11 billion in FY 2010–2011, or 9 percent of the total budget), as do a variety of other sources, including (all in FY 2010–2011): vehicle license fees (5.7 percent), fuel taxes (4.6 percent), insurance taxes (about 2 percent), and taxes on tobacco and alcohol (1 percent). The remainder comes from fees and fines imposed on a wide range of activities (parking at state parks, underground fuel storage, professional licensing,

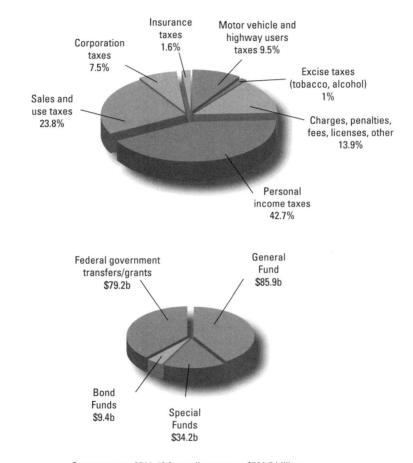

State revenue 2011-12 from all sources = $208.7 billion

FIGURE 8.1

State Revenue, 2011–12

Sources: California State Controller, California Department of Finance, http://www.ebudget.ca.gov.

Note: Percentages are based on general fund and special funds that were projected to generate $120.4 billion.

and so forth), rental income on state property, and surcharges on energy and other commerce (totaling approximately 13 percent).

Apart from taxation, state **borrowing** to plug budget holes and to finance mega-projects has become so commonplace that the average bond measure is in the $5 billion range,[1] and the state now carries $90 billion in bonded debt, excluding billions more that have been authorized and will be issued in the coming years. Most of the debt comes from voter-approved general obligation bonds dedicated to school construction and remodeling, public transportation projects (including a record-setting $19.9 billion omnibus transportation bill approved in 2006), and environmental and natural resource projects such as beach restoration and flood control. These measures veer sharply from the "pay-as-you-go" schemes typically used to finance large infrastructure projects in the past. Compared to the ten most populous states, California's debt burden is surpassed only by New York's. For example, in 2010 California's debt per capita was $2,362, compared to $520 in Texas (the lowest among large states), and $3,135 in New York. If debt is measured as a percent of the state's overall gross domestic product, the rate in California was 4.73 percent, whereas in Texas it was 1.05 percent, and 5.36 percent in New York. Extremely low ratings from the nation's independent credit rating agencies drive up costs by forcing the state to borrow at higher interest rates, adding billions more to the state's bond repayment obligations.

Mechanics of Budgeting: Deficits and Expenditures

The state commits to a spending plan before it knows how much will actually arrive in the state coffers. Legislative and Department of Finance analysts do their best to predict how much unemployment benefits, welfare, housing assistance, health coverage, and a host of other services will be needed, but the costs of these services depend on how the economic winds blow. A struggling economy typically means more residents lose jobs and fewer income taxes are paid; financially distressed consumers spend less and the state collects fewer sales taxes. Meanwhile, the state has already committed to a spending plan, but government expenses in the form of unemployment checks, health coverage, and other social services spike during economic hard times, and these imbalances translate into billions of dollars that policymakers cannot quickly replace. In one year alone (2008 to 2009), the state's collections for three major taxes—personal income, retail sales, and corporate—declined *$12.1 billion.*[2]

When expenses exceed revenues, **deficits** result. Legislators and governors must return to the negotiating table to reconcile the differences, or "close the budget gap," which can be accomplished through reducing benefit checks, cutting state workers' salaries and/or benefits, eliminating or reducing services, changing tax policies, borrowing, or a combination of any of these. State representatives have relied on all available options, including borrowing billions to cover portions of the state deficit during the 2000s, taking advantage of temporary federal stimulus funds beginning in 2009 ($85 billion in total, parceled out over several years across state, local, and nonprofit agencies), slicing state programs by billions of dollars (over $14 billion in cuts negotiated in spring 2011 alone), and resorting to "gimmicks" such as unrealistically assuming a much higher employment rate or that California will collect more in taxes. Governor Jerry Brown rejected some of these tactics in June 2011 by vetoing the budget for the first time in state history, calling it "unbalanced" and citing "legally questionable maneuvers, costly borrowing and unrealistic savings."[3] This angered fellow Democratic legislators and caused a constitutional brawl over whether lawmakers could receive their salaries while the budget sat in limbo.

What does the state pay for? **Education** dominates the budget, and funding levels for this area are typically locked in through initiatives and statutes. For example, except in times of fiscal emergency, Proposition 98 mandates a minimum spending threshold that usually results in 40 percent of the budget being dedicated to K–12 schools and community colleges, systems that include 6.3 million schoolchildren and 2.9 million full- and part-time community college students. Annual K–12 per-pupil spending dropped about $1,100 between 2000 and 2010 to about $7,900 per student, placing California at the bottom among state rankings.[4] Spending on the two major public university systems, California State University and the University of California, is not included in Prop 98, and their funding has also sharply decreased, despite total enrollment of about 630,000 students. The FY 2011–2012 budget alone stripped $650 million from *each* university system, with automatic triggers for another $650 million from each system if tax revenue did not materialize by January 1, 2012. All told, California spends about $45 billion on education annually.

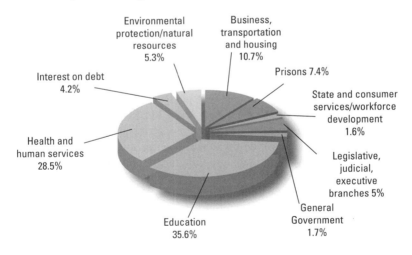

FIGURE 8.2

State Expenses, 2011–2012

Source: California Department of Finance, www.ebudget.ca.gov/home.htm.

Note: Percentages are based on combined general, special, and bond fund expenditures of $129.5 billion. Total state expenditures were projected to be $208.7 billion, including $120.4 billion in general and special funds, $9.4 in bond funds, and $79.2 billion in federal transfers and grants.

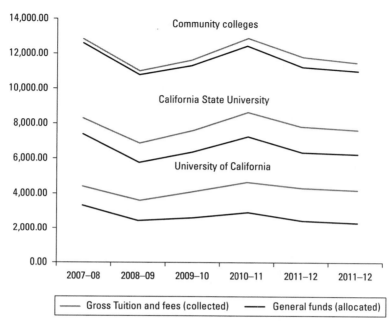

FIGURE 8.3

Budgeting for Higher Education Programs in California, 2007–2012

Note: These figures do not include state lottery funds or ARRA funds provided from 2009 to 2011. Excludes external sources of funding such as private grants and contracts.

Note: Additional automatic cuts amounting to $1.5 billion to each university system would be triggered if projected state revenues did not accrue by January 1, 2012.

Note: Gross tuition receipts are the total amount collected, including set-asides for financial aid.

Health and human services compete with education for the largest slice of the budget pie, representing almost 30 percent of the general fund in 2010–2011 and totaling almost $38 billion including special funds and bond funds. This category encompasses a range of essential services such as Medi-Cal, food stamps, residential care for the elderly, health care for children, and benefits for the unemployed and disabled. About one out of every five dollars spent by the state goes to Medi-Cal alone. To help meet the state's needs, the federal government transfers billions of dollars in welfare and other payments to the state, which are redistributed through state agencies and coordinated through state agencies like the Department of Health and Human Services.[5]

The state spends about $12.5 billion on **business, housing, and transportation**, including CalTrans and the California Highway Patrol, though much of that is derived from special funds and bond money. State government also incurs **general operational** costs: about $6 billion is spent to run the state's judicial, legislative, and executive offices, which contain eighteen thousand personnel positions (because some jobs are shared, there are actually more people employed).

Finally, at least another $9 billion goes to fund **prisons**, covering inmate medical care and rehabilitation programs, as well as prison guard salaries and operating costs. On average it costs California about $49,000 annually per adult inmate and more than $200,000 for each juvenile offender.

Political Constraints on Budgeting

The budgeting process is far more than a series of steps. By nature it is political, involving many factors that condition and constrain policymakers' ability to make collective decisions. These factors help explain how budgets can be late and out-of-balance by billions of dollars within weeks of their passage.

Above all, the budget reflects the **larger economic climate**. All state governments suffer the same economic challenges when the U.S. economy falters. Recessions decimate revenue sources such as personal income and sales taxes, which happen to be California's top two largest sources of revenue. Moreover, the state's tax policies have recently shifted some of the tax burden from corporations to individuals onto high-income individuals who largely rely on volatile earnings from capital gains and businesses. The top 15.6 percent of taxpayers (those 2.3 million making more than $100,000 per year) paid 83.6 percent of all personal income taxes in 2008. *The top 1 percent of taxpayers paid 43 percent of the state's income taxes*, including the contributions of about eighty billionaires who live in the state. Thus, the entire state budget critically depends on the financial fortunes of this small group (about forty-two thousand people making over $450,000 a year).[6]

The **political climate** also influences what kinds of programs receive funding and how much. Public opinion shifts and public pressure cause some issues to gain political traction. In the 1990s crime dominated the political agenda; it could be education or health care in another year. Furthermore, to the extent that lawmakers know who the loyal voters are and respond to them, biases will result in their privileging some "special" issues—and interests—over others.

Special interests and their lobbyists also unduly prevail throughout the process. Not only do they actively "educate" legislators about the effects of proposed budget changes, they also threaten to use the initiative process to achieve what legislators may not deliver. Special interest groups are behind some of the **ballot-box budgeting** that impedes legislators' flexibility: several initiatives already guarantee funding levels for such areas as education (Proposition 98), and it was a coalition of local governments that forced changes in state budgeting practices (Proposition 1A). Business and union lobbyists vigorously promote their own companies, workers, industries, and causes, but among the most active advocates in California are those who work for subgovernments of the type described in chapter 6, "stakeholders" that include schools, counties, cities, and special districts. All send swarms of policy experts and lobbyists to press their cases to the state lawmakers, who help determine how much money they will receive and how it must be spent.

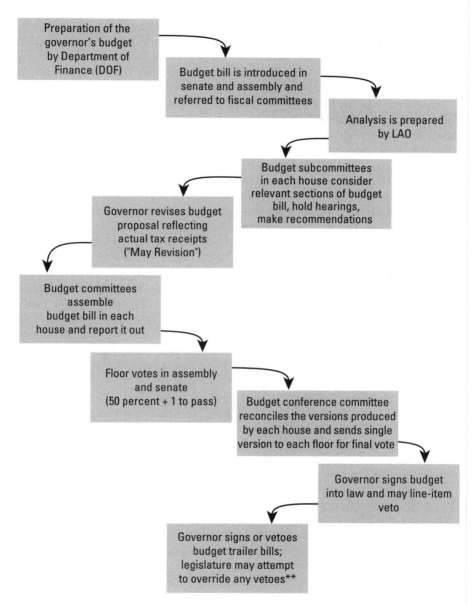

FIGURE 8.4

The Annual Budget Process

* More **typically, the senate and assembly leaders debate and negotiate with the governor** over final figures, with their staff members working overtime. If a conference committee meets, usually three people from each house participate. From this point, **permutations of the process occur with regularity.**

** Leaders in each house help members construct many separate, omnibus **"budget trailer bills" that contain new policies or formalize legal changes** reflected in the final budget figures. Trailer bills are processed through the houses, and the governor signs (or vetoes) each one. The legislature may attempt to override the governor's vetoes, but achieving the two-thirds threshold is rare.

Term limits also contribute to the tangle by continually stocking and restocking the legislature with many novice lawmakers who lack big-picture understanding of how systems in the state interrelate and how cuts in one area will affect others. It takes more than one budget cycle to gain a working understanding of how the process itself unfolds, and much longer to grasp how different constituencies are affected by changes.

Citizens' use of the ballot box has fundamentally reshaped budgeting practices throughout the state as well. **Proposition 13** is a case in point. Prior to 1978, cities, counties, and schools relied on property taxes to finance their budgets. When Prop 13 capped property taxes at 1 percent of a home's or commercial building's purchase price and limited property assessment increases to no more than 2 percent per year, local governments were forced to look for other ways to pay for services (now mainly sales taxes and fees), and state government assumed responsibility for refilling local government accounts and funding schools. However, when times got tough, as they did in the early 1990s, the state substantially changed the way it allocated education funds, resulting in the redirection of yet more revenues away from local governments. Since then, state lawmakers have adopted the practice of occasionally "borrowing" property taxes from local jurisdictions to pay for schools or simply to plug large holes in the state budget. Thus, the burden of low property taxes has been shared by local governments, which have struggled to find alternative sources of revenue, and the state government, which cannot meet its obligations to fund local governments and schools when the general fund is empty and consequently still "owes" billions to local governments and schools.

In all of this, **rules matter**. Majority party legislators are hamstrung by the **two-thirds supermajority vote requirement to raise taxes and fees**, which has required majority Democrats to seek votes from the minority party—a nearly impossible task. Unless fifty-four assembly members and twenty-seven senators are willing to hike sales taxes or vehicle license fees, for example, the majority party will need several minority party members' votes to implement an increase. The only exception involves the risky move of including one or more fee hikes in the budget itself, which only requires a simple majority vote for approval.[7]

Until 2010 one rule mattered most above all others: the two-thirds vote requirement for passing the budget. Because of their power to control the budget vote, minority party members regarded the budget as their only opportunity to meaningfully influence public policy and force the majority to meet their demands. Over the past few years, long delays have resulted from the parties' inability to reconcile fundamental political differences (in 2010 the budget was one hundred days overdue), compelled by the minority Republicans' stand-pat refusal to compromise on tax increases and the majority Democrats' opposition to cutting certain services. In 2010 Californians lowered the threshold for passing the budget to a simple majority, meaning 50 percent plus one (forty-one assembly members and twenty-one senators), thus shifting the burden of constructing a balanced budget to the Democratic majority. In tough economic times this is easier said than done, however, as the majority party must make and take the blame for cuts to social services that people demand. They could avoid cuts by raising taxes, but this is again a nearly hopeless option, which further complicates the (Democratic) majority party's task.

Generally speaking, representatives would rather give their constituents what they want rather than risk losing the next election because they "caused" their constituents to lose an important state service such as in-home elderly care for an aging mother, or receive a lower unemployment check, or lose health care coverage, or be unable to find day care for a child whose school year was cut short. Thus, **risk-averse politicians** who may be trying to promote the general welfare but shy away from making painful cuts help drive up deficits. This underlies the phenomenon of giant **structural budget deficits** after 2000 that were created by long-term commitments to programs that were initially paid for with increases in revenues that later disappeared. In other words, lawmakers used higher revenues from the "dot-com boom" to play catch-up with major programs that had been neglected or underfunded for years, but they found it difficult to reduce spending levels when revenue sources dried up. Deficits have been carried over from previous years, further widening budget gaps and underscoring the fact that every budget builds on the prior one. Until baseline spending is brought in line with revenues, those imbalances will persist as a "structural budget gap."

Tax Burden: Highest in the Nation?

It is a common complaint among Californians that they pay more in taxes than the average residents of other U.S. states. California's ranking in terms of overall state and local debt burden tends to justify that view: according to at least one source, the state placed fifteenth among the fifty states in 2010.[8] However, if state and local revenues are considered as a share of economic wealth or income, the state's ranking is considerably lower.[9] The state's nonpartisan Legislative Analyst's Office calls the overall burden "somewhat above average" based on its calculation of state and local taxes: $11.66 per $100 of personal income, just above the national U.S. average of $10.99.[10]

In combination with local sales taxes, the one-cent temporary increase to the state sales tax in 2010–2011 placed California ahead of all others in that category, though it expired in June 2011, returning the base rate to 7.25%—still among the highest in the nation.[11] However, thanks to Proposition 13, individual property taxes remain relatively low and place the state near the bottom in rankings in that category.[12] Corporate taxes and personal income taxes place it near, but not at, the top, whereas comparatively low "sin" taxes on alcohol and tobacco once more place it near the bottom. For example, as of 2011 California ranked thirty-third in cigarette taxes, twenty-fourth in beer taxes ($0.20 per gallon), and was almost the lowest ranked state for table wine taxes ($0.20 per gallon, the same as Texas and only slightly higher than Louisiana's $.11 per gallon. By comparison, both Florida and Alaska impose taxes of more than $2 per gallon).[13]

On an individual basis, whether Californians pay more or less than taxpayers in other states depends greatly on which tax is being considered, how much a person earns, homeowner status, regional location, and what goods and services that person consumes. These factors also influence the perception of being overtaxed at least as much as a person's attitudes about public spending and the proper role of government do.

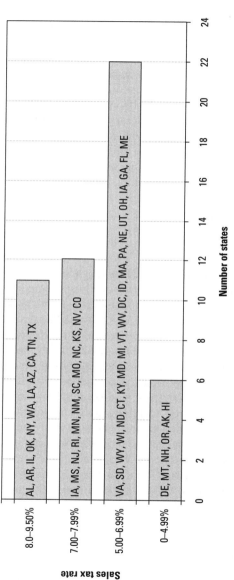

FIGURE 8.5

Combined State and Average Local Tax Rates as of July 1, 2011

Note: Some states levy gross receipts taxes in addition to sales taxes.

Note: These figures include the base tax rate for the state combined with the average local tax rate in the state.

Source: Tax Foundation calculations (based on 2010 U.S. Census, Sales Tax Clearinghouse), www.taxfoundation.org.

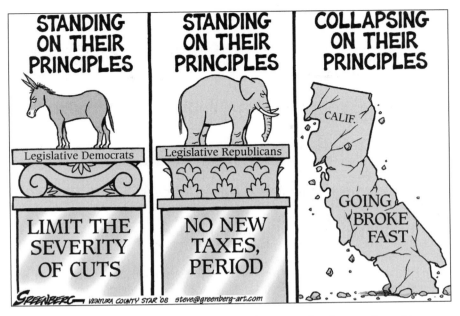

STANDING ON THEIR PRINCIPLES

Legislative Democrats

LIMIT THE SEVERITY OF CUTS

STANDING ON THEIR PRINCIPLES

Legislative Republicans

NO NEW TAXES, PERIOD

COLLAPSING ON THEIR PRINCIPLES

CALIF.

GOING BROKE FAST

GREENBERG — VENTURA COUNTY STAR '08   steve@greenberg-art.com

Yet when it comes to budgeting, not enough revenue has been collected to cover all that Californians appear to collectively want. Solid majorities oppose spending cuts to education and health and human services, but fewer than half support higher sales taxes or vehicle license fees, and the only category of cuts citizens would support is in prisons and corrections—a category that the federal courts have determined is already grossly *under*funded.[14] However, it is worth noting that while Californians seem to have a penchant for keeping taxes low, time and again it has been shown that while they oppose general tax increases, they are much more willing to support specific taxes if the funds are designated for specific purposes.

Conclusion: Budgeting under Duress

As a U.S. state, California faces most of the same basic challenges as the other forty-nine, but as one of the world's largest countries, its economy is intimately tied to global fortunes, and its fiscal dilemmas are comparable in scope and depth. The sheer volume of issues generated by its more than thirty-eight million residents is staggering, and the majority of those issues are reflected, though not always resolved, in the state's annual budgets. National and international crises can trigger severe and unanticipated drop-offs in tax revenues and no realistic way to immediately cut services without undermining the government's legal commitments. The ability of policymakers to manage budget crises is strongly conditioned by factors outside their control, but their behavior is also incentivized by rules such as supermajority votes or the potential loss of pay. As recent budget meltdowns, delays, and austere spending cuts illustrate, effective governing demands rules that facilitate rather than obstruct compromise. Avoiding economic catastrophe depends on it.

Notes

1. Ellen Hanak, "Paying for Infrastructure: California's Choices," Public Policy Institute of California, January 2009, http://www.ppic.org/content/pubs/atissue/AI_109EHAI.pdf.

2. California State Controller's Office, www.sco.ca.gov/Press-Releases/2009/07–09summary.pdf.

3. Shane Goldmacher and Anthony York, "Governor Vetoes 'Unbalanced' State Budget," *Los Angeles Times*, June 17, 2011, http://articles.latimes.com/2011/jun/17/local/la-me-0617-state-budget-20110617.

4. The number is based on 2009–2010 inflation-adjusted figures provided by legislative analyst Mac Taylor in "Cal Facts, January 2011," www.lao.ca.gov/reports/2011/calfacts/calfacts_010511.pdf.

5. Compare figures from both the Department of Finance ("Chart B, Historical Data, Budget Expenditures," July 2011, www.dof.ca.gov/budgeting/budget_faqs/documents/CHART-B.pdf) and the U.S. Census Bureau, which pegs the dollar amount of transfers to California at $53.8 billion in 2008. See Statistical Abstract of the United States, Table 431, "Federal Aid to State and Local Governments by State: 2000–2008" (p. 269), www.census.gov/compendia/statab/2011/tables/11s0431.pdf.

6. Figures are from the California Tax Franchise Board for the most recent tax year available, 2008. See 2009 Annual Report, Table B-4A.1, "Personal Income Tax Statistics for Resident Tax Returns." www.ftb.ca.gov/aboutFTB/Tax_Statistics/Reports/Personal_Income_Tax/2009_B-4A.pdf.

7. The majority Democrats raised vehicle license fees an additional $12 through the 2011–2012 budget without the approval of Republicans. Because the simple majority vote threshold was implemented by Proposition 25 in 2010, it remains to be seen whether the tactic will hold up in court, because it may conflict with Proposition 26 (also approved on the same ballot), requiring virtually all "fee" increases be approved by a two-thirds supermajority vote in the legislature.

8. Data taken from Tax Foundation, "State Sales, Gasoline, Cigarette, and Alcohol Taxes, July 1, 2009, www.taxfoundation.org/files/state_various_sales_rates-20090701.pdf.

9. Tracy Gordon, "California Budget," Public Policy Institute of California, July 2009.

10. Based on the most recent figures available, 2007–2008, for the January 2011 publication of "Cal Facts" by the Legislative Analyst's Office.

11. The base sales rate returned to 7.25% on July 1, 2011, despite Jerry Brown's efforts to bring the tax extensions to the voters through a special election. He promised to place the issue before voters again in 2012, despite Republican opposition and the real possibility that voters would reject this increase—along with other proposed tax hikes.

12. Tax Foundation, "State Tax and Spending Policy," www.taxfoundation.org/taxdata/topic/9.html.

13. Source: Federation of Tax Administrators, "State Excise Taxes," January 1, 2011, http://www.taxadmin.org/Fta/rate/tax_stru.html#Excise.

14. According to the PPIC's May 2011 "Californians and their Government" survey, "When asked about cutting spending to help reduce the state budget deficit, solid majorities of adults and likely voters oppose cuts in three of the four largest budget categories: K–12 public education (76% adults, 73% likely voters), higher education (68% adults, 64% likely voters) or health and human services (66% adults, 61% likely voters). But they support cuts in the fourth category: prisons and corrections (62% adults, 70% likely voters)." These statistics are roughly mirrored in past state surveys that ask similar or the same questions. See http://www.ppic.org/content/pubs/survey/S_511MBS.pdf.

CHAPTER 9

Political Parties, Elections, and Campaigns

Political scientist E. E. Schattschneider wrote in 1942 that "modern democracies are unthinkable save in terms of political parties,"[1] and the same can be said of elections. Without parties, the scale and scope of conflict produced by countless disorganized groups would be unmanageable. Without elections, citizens would lack the means to hold their representatives accountable. Through both parties and elections, diverse interests are voiced, aggregated, and translated into policy.

Many Californians remain unconvinced. Fully three-quarters of voters believe that state government is run by a few big interests, and majorities across parties think they make better public policy decisions than elected officials do.[2] Most voters are at least fairly satisfied with an initiative process that allows them to bypass a state government they generally despise—though less than half (44 percent) trust their fellow voters to make public policy at the ballot box. The "decline to state" or independent voter category is the only one to have sustained an upward climb since 1980, surpassing the 20 percent mark in 2009. A higher percentage—over one-third—of registered voters aged 18–34 refuse to affiliate with either of the two major parties. Turnout consistently remains low among Latinos, the state's largest ethnic group.

Political communities define themselves by how they use parties and elections, and these facts shed light on California's independent streak, its complex electorate, and

113

its antigovernment political culture. Two other defining features of California's political landscape are also worth noting upfront, both of which have important implications for governing. The first is an **east-west divide** that has opened along liberal-conservative lines, whereby the coastal regions are heavily liberal to moderate and trend Democratic, and inland counties are much more conservative and strongly Republican. The second is that **citizens, residents, and voters are not the same groups of people.** Reasons for these trends and their impacts are discussed in this chapter, along with the style of California parties, the character of elections, and the conduct of campaigns.

A Weak Party State

Historically speaking, political parties in California have struggled for survival, not prospered. Much of their troubles date to Progressive reforms in the early twentieth century deliberately designed to strip them of their power. Idealizing politics without partisanship, Progressives overhauled election law by establishing new mechanisms for voters to sidestep parties altogether—the initiative, referendum, and recall being foremost among these. Other innovations included nonpartisan elections for local elections and judges and cross-filing at the state level for statewide elected officials (discussed in chapter 2). Through secret ballots, direct primaries, and banning parties from endorsing candidates prior to elections, party members were able to choose their nominees without the blessing of party bosses.

A good deal of the Progressives' antiparty program flourishes today. Cross-filing was eliminated long ago,[3] but the long-term consequences of the Progressives' attack on parties are still visible: voters split their tickets between Republicans and Democrats for different offices, state party organizations remain relatively weak, and candidates tend to self-select and draw on their own resources rather than those of their party. One of every five registered California voters is in the "decline to state" category, having registered with no party at all.

Parties are far from ineffective in the state, however, and they continue to thrive within government. Minority-party Republicans have held their ground against raising taxes in order to balance the budget, and majority-party Democrats have retaliated by refusing to pass Republican members' bills and standing firm against cutting services they consider essential. The goals, values, and agendas of the two parties remain far apart. Yet, on balance, the evidence supports the judgment that California remains a weak party state. This can also be seen by examining more systematically the three interconnected parts of the party system: party *in the electorate* (PIE), *in government* (PIG), and *as an organization* (PO).

Party in the California Electorate

In one respect, a political party is made up of members who share similar beliefs about the role that government should play in their lives, but "party in the

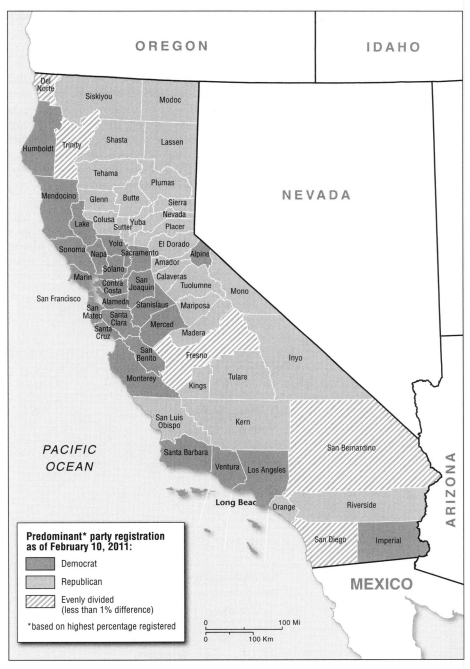

MAP 9.1

California's East-West Partisan Divide

electorate" also refers to the generalized sentiment a party's members share about what it means to be a Republican, Democrat, or member of any other party. It is this sentiment that leads them to vote for certain officials and reinforces their attachment to the party's "brand name."

Three-quarters of registered California voters belong to one of the two major parties, Republican and Democratic, but that number is somewhat deceiving. According to a recent statewide survey, a majority of Californians think the state needs a third political party, and seven out of ten say that they would prefer to be unaffiliated with any party.[4] Furthermore, because neither party has absolute majority status, independent voters provide the swing votes necessary to win in general elections. While California is commonly labeled a "blue state" based on registration statistics and statewide elections that have overwhelmingly favored Democrats, the influence of independents has turned its political complexion slightly purple.

In terms of party registration, California was a majority Democratic state between 1934 and 1989; since then this has been the state's plurality party, edging out Republicans by 13.1 percent in February 2011. Democrats today are first in registration at 44 percent, Republicans take second at 30.9 percent, and third parties

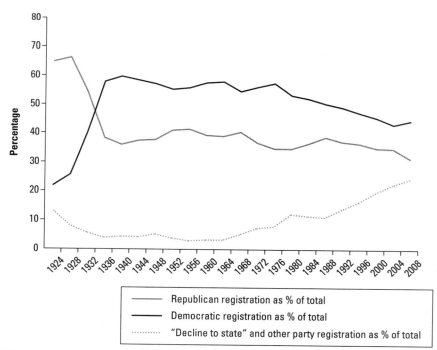

FIGURE 9.1

Party Registration in Presidential Election Years, 1924–2008

Note: The percentages reflect the statistics from the closing date for registration in the general election.

Source: California Secretary of State, Report of Registration, October 2008.

BOX 9.1 How to Party in California

To qualify as a new political party in California, a group must first hold a caucus or convention at which officers are elected and a name is chosen. Qualification may then proceed either by petition or by registration. Petitioners need to gather 1,030,040 signatures, a number equal to 10 percent of the total number of people who cast votes in the most previous gubernatorial (governor's) election, and they must file those petitions in several counties at least 135 days before the next election. The registration option requires that 103,004 persons (1 percent) complete an affidavit of registration at least 154 days prior to the next election—a difficult task to coordinate statewide.

Registered Parties in California:

- American Independent: www.aipca.org
- Democratic: www.cadem.org
- Green: www.cagreens.org
- Libertarian: www.ca.lp.org
- Peace and Freedom: www.peaceandfreedom.org
- Republican: www.cagop.org

Parties That Have Failed to Qualify:

- Anarchy and Poverty
- California Moderate
- Dharma
- God, Truth, and Love
- Humanitarian
- Pot
- Reform
- Superhappy Party
- United Conscious Builders of the Dream
- Utopia Manifesto Party

Source: California Secretary of State.

collectively hold third place with a combined membership of 4.7 percent. Individuals who affiliate with no party constitute 20.4 percent of the state's electorate.[5]

"Decline to state" voters include people who consider themselves politically independent, although political scientists have found that those who "lean" toward one party or the other usually vote for that party. Historically, independents cast more votes for Democrats in California elections. For example, exit polls showed that 56 percent of independents chose Democrat Jerry Brown over Republican Meg Whitman in the November 2010 governor's race, and 64 percent of independents voted for Obama in 2008, compared to 92 percent of Democrats and 14 percent of Republicans.[6]

Current members of the Democratic Party in California tend to be ethnically diverse, in the low-to-middle income bracket, and younger than in the past. About one out of two Democrats is Latino, African American, or Asian, and 54 percent are white.[7] About a third of Democrats have household incomes of $40,000 or less per year, and a quarter of them are renters rather than homeowners. Women also prefer the Democratic Party: approximately 16 percent more women than men are registered as Democrats.

Republicans, meanwhile, tend to be white and middle-to-upper class, and they count more evangelical Christians among their ranks. In contrast to Democrats, 82 percent are white, and men outnumber women in Republican Party registration by about four points. Majorities in both parties are college graduates, but a plurality of Republicans (47 percent) make $80,000 or more, compared to 38 percent of Democrats and 44 percent of independents. Republicans tend to be older, and nearly half are at least age fifty-five. By comparison, only 32 percent of independents are older than age fifty-four. On the whole, these statistics mirror nationwide trends in party registration.

About three out of four California Republicans describe themselves as **conservatives:** they generally want a government strictly limited in size, are more responsive to business than labor, do not believe in raising taxes, are strongly opposed to homosexual marriage, favor strong laws restricting illegal immigration, and believe that "individual destiny should be in the individual's hands."[8]

California Democrats, on the other hand, tend to hold **liberal** views: they would pay higher taxes in exchange for more government services, they want the government to promote equal opportunity in education and the workplace, they want greater access to health care, they favor pro-choice laws, and they are more responsive to labor than business. There is nearly universal belief among Democrats that immediate steps should be taken to curb the effects of global warming or climate

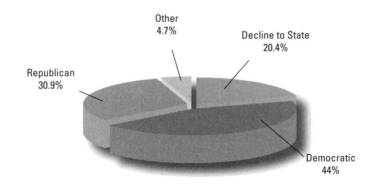

FIGURE 9.2

Registration by Political Party in California, 2011

Source: California Secretary of State, "Odd-Numbered Year Report of Registration, February 10, 2011," www.sos.ca.gov/elections/ror/ror-pages/ror-odd-year-11/.

change, compared to about half (54 percent) of Republicans who hold that view. Half of Democrats say they are liberal, and about a third consider themselves moderates. In contrast, **independents** are distributed widely across the ideological spectrum: most (40 percent) describe themselves as middle-of-the-road, and equal proportions (slightly less than one-third) consider themselves liberal or conservative.[9]

Party in Government

Those most responsible for advancing a party's brand name through policymaking are current elected officials: the party in government. Approximately twenty thousand officials in California hold elective office; of them, 132 hold statewide office and fifty-five represent Californians in the U.S. Congress. Governors, assembly members, senators, federal representatives, and others pursue agenda items that become associated with a party's name through fulfilling their chief purpose: *to organize government in order to achieve their policy aims.*

Democrats have held the title of majority party for forty years in both legislative houses. The assembly and senate have been majority Democrat almost continuously since 1971, interrupted only by Republican rule in the assembly from 1995 to 1996. A high degree of ideological polarization pervades the capitol, especially with regard to taxation and spending: Democrats are more willing to raise certain taxes and fees (the annual tax paid on cars or cigarette taxes, or income tax paid by millionaires for example), and Republicans are unwilling to raise them, period, and instead insist on cuts to social services.

This basic difference has exacerbated the parties' inability to pass budgets on time and is reflected in strong party solidarity and ideological rigidity. One explanation for that rigidity is found in strongly partisan districts where the election of a Democrat or a Republican is a foregone conclusion. In most districts the "real" competition takes place during the primaries among candidates of the same party vying for the votes of strong partisans, and more ideologically extreme candidates have tended to be favored under these circumstances. In recent decades almost no districts have switched parties from election to election: only two open seats switched hands in 2010, and none did in November 2008.

Why have districts been so uncompetitive? Reasons include *gerrymandering* and *natural sorting*. **Gerrymandering** refers to the act of manipulating district boundaries to include or exclude certain groups in order to benefit a party or an incumbent. Until 2010 the state lawmakers—in actuality, the majority Democrats—were in charge of redistricting and tended to draw maps that guaranteed a Democratic majority and few competitive seats. The 2000 cycle was considered a "bipartisan gerrymander" because both sides agreed to maintain the status quo with minimal regard to increasing competitiveness. This legislative branch-dominated process mirrors that which occurs in most U.S. states: thirty-six states leave the task of redrawing their own district boundaries to state lawmakers, whereas another twelve entrust redistricting authority to independent commissions.[10] Californians joined the latter category in 2008 through the passage of Proposition 11, which authorized an independent commission composed of citizens to take control of the redistricting process. Party leaders and legislators are now barred from playing an active role in forming their own districts following the 2010 census, though they are allowed to make the case to fourteen citizen mapmakers that respecting existing boundaries might help preserve consistency in representation, a due point for consideration—along all the others voiced by citizens from across the state.

Yet it can also be plausibly argued that the political geography of California reflects natural **sorting:** like-minded people tend to live near each other, and settlement patterns have produced a densely populated coastline that is more "blue" Democratic and an inland that is more "red" Republican. A less partisan redistricting process—such as the one promised by Prop 11—is unlikely to produce a slew of new competitive districts because mapmakers are still bound to draw districts containing numerically equal populations that are as compact as possible, respect city and county lines, and do not split communities of interest. These conditions pit practicality against ideals and, in the end, electoral interparty competition suffers. Regardless, citizens have been swayed by the argument that lawmakers in principle should not be in charge of drawing their own districts, whether or not more competitive districts are created.

The Democrats' stronghold has not extended to the governor's office, where Republicans have held the seat for almost fifty of nearly seventy years since World War II. They have also managed to secure other statewide executive offices

TABLE 9.1 Modern Era California Governors by Party Affiliation

Term (years)	Governor	Party affiliation
1943–1954 (12)	Earl Warren	Republican*
1955–1958 (4)	Goodwin Knight	Republican
1959–1966 (8)	Edmund "Pat" Brown	Democrat
1967–1974 (8)	Ronald Reagan	Republican
1975–1982 (8)	Edmund "Jerry" Brown Jr.	Democrat
1983–1990 (8)	George Deukmejian	Republican
1991–1998 (8)	Pete Wilson	Republican
1999–2003 (5)	Gray Davis	Democrat
2003–2010 (8)	Arnold Schwarzenegger	Republican
2011–present	Edmund "Jerry" Brown Jr.	Democrat

*Warren also received the nomination of the Democratic Party.

over the decades, preventing Democrats from monopolizing state administrative power.

The Party Organizations

Finally, the concept of party encompasses organizational bodies and their rules. It should be noted that when citizens register to vote they actually become members of their *state* parties, organized according to election law in the fifty different states and the District of Columbia. This is why voter registration forms are addressed to a country registrar of voters rather than a national party association, and voters are given the option to register when they visit the Department of Motor Vehicles (DMV), a state agency. The national organizations known as the Democratic National Committee and Republican National Committee have little to no control over the state parties.

Party organizations are well suited to fulfill another key party role: that of *nominating candidates for election and getting them elected.* At the top is the party **state central committee**, responsible for coordinating the local bodies that exist below it, for strategizing to win seats, and for assisting candidates with funding and other resources. These committees run the respective state conventions every year.

A state party chair acts as "CEO" of the party, and members of the state central committees include current statewide elected officials, nominees for statewide office, county-level party officials, and appointed and elected members from across the state. Democratic members of their state central committee number 2,900, evenly divided between men and women. There are approximately 1,530 members (no gender quotas) of the Republican state central committee. Beneath the major state party organs are fifty-eight **county central committees** for each party, also organized by the state election codes. Further down are volunteer local regional clubs that are home to a few activists but not many members.

Elections: Continuity and Change

Like political parties, elections are a keystone of democracy, and voters continue to find ways to improve them, usually in order to address what is perceived as unfair advantages. Major initiatives periodically target the role of parties and the conduct of candidates in elections by readjusting the rules for citizens, parties, incumbents, and candidates. One such change could take effect for the 2016 presidential elections: how California allocates its Electoral College votes for U.S. president. Under the U.S. Constitution, each state determines how it will cast its electoral votes. In order to avoid the dilemma that arises when a candidate receives the U.S. popular vote but loses the election, as was the case with Al Gore in 2000, California will now direct its electors to cast its votes for the presidential candidate who wins the most popular votes in the U.S. The plan will take effect only when enough states enact this "national popular vote" law (collectively they must possess 270 electoral college votes, a simple majority). California is the ninth state to implement this revision.

The other extremely significant change in recent times was the imposition of term limits on elected state officials in 1990, which generated a slew of electoral consequences. For one, the game of political office "musical chairs" now extends to all levels of government: competition for "downticket" offices such as county boards of supervisors and big-city mayors has increased, and pitched contests over congressional seats have also multiplied as the pool of experienced candidates looking for a job continues to swell. About two-thirds of all statewide officials attempt to run for another office within two years of being termed out. It's also fairly common now for incumbents to be challenged by members of their own party—rivalries that used to be adroitly managed by party leaders or preempted by the advantages of incumbency that scared off good challengers (those with experience and money). Competition between and among incumbents has been exacerbated by redistricting carried out without regard for where the incumbents reside. Ironically, term limits have not affected incumbents' chances for reelection, however; officeholders continue to be reelected at near-perfect rates. Not one incumbent state legislator was defeated in 2010.

Special elections to fill vacant seats are also on the rise due to term limits, as politicians leave one office for another when it becomes available. This tends to create a "domino effect," which occurs when a state senator runs for an open U.S. Congress seat and a member of the assembly then runs for the subsequently vacated state senate seat. This then creates a third election needed to fill the empty assembly seat and so on down the line. Between June 2010 and July 2011, no fewer than twelve special primary and general elections were held to fill congressional or state legislative seats, most of which were vacated by ambitious elected officials. Separately, governors or the legislature may also call special statewide elections so that voters can consider measures of great urgency. Governor Schwarzenegger did not find special elections to be a particularly helpful vehicle for building political support, however, as an irritated electorate rejected every one of his proposals in special elections held in 2005 and 2009. Unfortunately for cash-strapped California, the average price tag for statewide special elections can approach $100 million, and voter turnout can be dismally low.[11] Barely 21 percent of eligible voters cast ballots in the special election held in May 2009—the lowest in state history for a statewide election. Special general elections for legislative seats drew an average 23 percent turnout from 1991 to 2011.

In addition to term limits, at least three other noteworthy reforms are reshaping California elections. First, the failings of punch-card systems laid bare by the 2000 presidential election between Vice President Al Gore and Texas governor George W. Bush prompted the U.S. Congress to pass the Help America Vote Act of 2002. Every state received millions of dollars to replace older voting equipment with more accurate touch-screen and optical-scan machines. California's secretary of state, who has

Democratic senator Leland Yee joins supporters at the capitol in Sacramento to celebrate his election to the state senate in 2006, which made him the first Chinese American to serve in that chamber.

overseen the transition away from punch-card devices, monitors the new equipment for software glitches and intentional mischief. All counties are now outfitted with advanced voting technology—the need for which is increasingly offset by the registered California voters who "vote by mail" or are "permanent absentee" voters. Approximately 55 percent of voters cast mail ballots in the 2010 midterm election, and more than one-third of voters have "permanent absentee voter" status (meaning they only receive and submit their ballots through the mail)—a figure that has doubled since 2004.

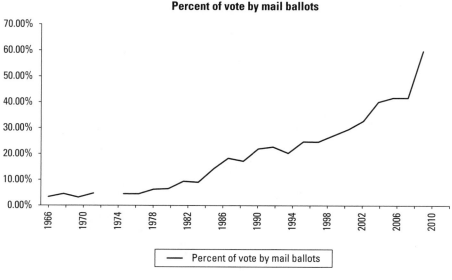

Percent of vote by mail ballots

— Percent of vote by mail ballots

FIGURE 9.3

Vote by Mail Statistics, 1966–2010

Note: Data was not collected for 1974.

Source: California Secretary of State, "Historical Vote-By-Mail (Absentee) Ballot Use in California," www.sos.ca.gov/elections/hist_absentee.htm.

Second, and more importantly, for years reformers have tried to pry open primary elections to allow greater participation by the entire electorate. In **primary elections**, party members nominate candidates for various offices that then will go on to compete head to head with the other party's nominees in the general election. For instance, six Republicans may jump into an assembly primary race, but only one will receive enough votes to become the Republican nominee for the assembly seat, and incumbents invariably receive their party's renomination. That person will later face the Democratic nominee in the November **general election**.

Until 1996 the state had a **closed primary** system, meaning that only voters who declared their party affiliation prior to the election could participate in their own party's election. At the voting station a voter would receive a Republican or a Democratic ballot listing party candidates for each office. Independent or "decline to state" voters could not participate in the nomination elections, though they could vote on statewide initiatives, local measures, or nonpartisan offices.

Proposition 198 (1996) changed the rules, but only temporarily. Californians approved the **blanket primary**, in which all registered voters could vote for any

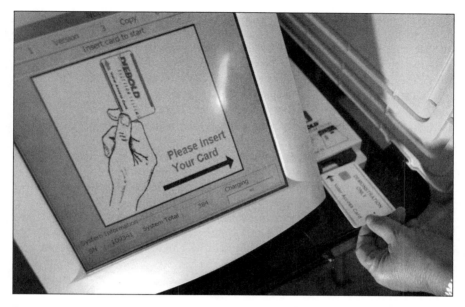

Touch-screen systems have been certified for use in every California county, though some counties use optical-scan machines that require voters to fill in bubbles on a paper ballot that is then electronically scanned.

candidate. In 1998 primary election voters were given a single ballot listing each office and every possible candidate for it, just as in a general election. Two years later the U.S. Supreme Court ruled the scheme an unconstitutional violation of political parties' First Amendment right to free association. A **modified closed primary** took its place, and "decline to state" voters could have their votes counted if a party authorized it. In June 2010 California voters decided again to switch to an **open primary**. In exchange for his vote to pass the budget in 2009, Republican senator Abel Maldonado demanded the legislature place a constitutional amendment on the ballot creating a **"top-two candidate"** open primary system, in which any registered voter may select a top choice from among all candidates for office. Unless one candidate receives a majority of all votes cast for that office, the top two winners advance to the general election for a run-off, be they two Republicans, two Democrats, one from each party, or otherwise. Reformers hoped to simultaneously encourage the election of moderate candidates who would need to appeal to a wider electorate and to deter the selection of ideologically polarizing figures. Because Democrats hold the advantage in state voter registration, the scheme is expected to pit more Democratic candidates against each other in general elections.

A third significant catalyst for electoral change is the set of redistricted maps produced by the Citizens Redistricting Commission. Newly drawn boundaries for the 2012 elections have forced many of California's representatives into the same districts, which has caused several to move their residences into neighboring districts where they might avoid a standoff with a colleague. Seeing that long and friendly relationships among incumbents have been disrupted, new challengers have entered the fray (a development that the initiative's proponents undoubtedly have welcomed). The 2012 redistricting cycle will redefine the odds for some incumbents and prospective challengers, though it will likely take a couple of election cycles before political scientists can discern redistricting's electoral consequences, such as whether more moderate candidates benefit from the new system.

One additional reform will soon change the way Californians register to vote and, possibly, the outcomes of elections. Under a law signed by Governor Brown in October 2011, an online voter registration process should be in place prior to the November 2012 elections. Electronic or online registration processes already exist in eleven other states, such as Kansas and Arizona, and have been shown to increase voter registration rates.

California Campaigns

Given parties' relatively weak hold over Californians, the frequency of elections, a mobile population, and the immense size and density of districts, campaigns serve the important role of connecting citizens with candidates and incumbents. Across the state, virtually all campaigners face the same basic challenges: raising huge sums of cash to buy access to potential voters and convincing enough of those voters to reject their opponents.

Former assembly Speaker Jesse Unruh once proclaimed that "Money is the mother's milk of politics."[12] Indeed, incumbents cannot afford to stop raising money, waging what is known as the nonstop "permanent campaign." On average, a successful assembly campaign costs about $750,000, and a senate campaign can easily run more than $1 million.[13] But those costs critically depend on how strong the competition is: incumbents running in a general election usually face "sacrificial lambs" that spend almost nothing in their defense, whereas some incumbents without serious challengers still spend in excess of $1.5 million "defending" their seats.

Open-seat elections, created regularly now by term limits, require far higher sums. Candidates for open assembly seats spend an average of $950,000; the most exorbitant races can cost candidates over $3 million. Costs are also higher when there is a possibility that the other party could win the seat: two senate candidates in 2008 spent a combined sum of more than $8.5 million, and the winner squeaked by with 857 votes.

Among the largest and most frequent contributors to campaigns are trade unions, energy companies, the state parties, candidates who give to each other, ideological or single-issue groups, and business associations. Tribal governments, ranked among the largest groups of donors in 2008, dramatically curtailed their

TABLE 9.2 Largest Campaign Contributors to State Campaigns by Industry, 2010

Industry	Contributions
Electric utilities; oil & gas:	$69,193,656
Public sector unions:	$45,425,102
Communications & electronics:	$29,875,014
General business (food, hotel, alcohol, manufacturing, tobacco, recreation, tourism, etc.):	$29,452,074
General trade unions:	$28,662,009
Party committees:	$24,610,947

Source: Followthemoney.org, www.followthemoney.org/database/StateGlance/state_contributors.phtml?s=CA&y=2010.

spending in 2010 (to $6 million, down from $163 million). Out-of-state contributors also donate multiple millions, though all donors are subject to limits on money that may be given directly to candidates. The only exception is that candidates enjoy the constitutional right to spend as much of their own money as they wish.

All campaign contributions and expenditures must be reported to the California secretary of state's office, which makes fund-raising activity publicly available pursuant to Proposition 9 (see http://cal-access.ss.ca.gov). However, the rules changed considerably with the U.S. Supreme Court ruling in *Citizens United v. Federal Election Commission* (2010), which lifted a seventy-year-old ban on independent expenditures by corporations and unions in the name of free speech. Large sums are now being spent in state and federal campaigns without strict reporting and disclosure requirements, principally in the form of mass mailings and television and radio ads designed to defeat or endorse candidates (without the candidate's knowledge).

Why do candidates require so much campaign funding? In districts as large as those found in California, paid media are the only way to reach large swaths of potential voters. Most candidates in the state invest heavily in **retail campaigning,** the kind that takes place through broadcast advertising and direct mail. These two types of retail activities dominate the statewide elections and are costly, particularly in urban media markets where the airwaves are already crowded with commercial ads. Professional campaign managers and consultants help candidates build efficient money-raising machines by coordinating other critical aspects of successful campaigns: access to donors, polling data, media buys, Web-based tools, targeted messages, and volunteers.

This is not to say that knocking on doors, attending community events, and "pressing the flesh"—types of **wholesale** campaigning that require a comfortable pair of shoes rather than large amounts of campaign cash—are unimportant in modern campaigns. Personal contact is particularly beneficial in local contests in which friends and neighbors help turn out the vote.

EBay president and CEO Meg Whitman broke campaign records in her bid for the California governorship against Jerry Brown when she spent $144 million of her own fortune on the race. Including funds she raised, Whitman's campaign spent a total of $178.5 million compared to Brown's $36.7 million. The second woman in California history (and the first Republican woman) to make it to the general gubernatorial election, Whitman lost the election with 40.9% to Brown's 53.8%. For Whitman, that works out to $43.25 spent per vote, and $6.75 for Brown.

Conclusion: A Complex Electorate

Parties, elections, and campaigns have been the instruments of change and the targets of reform. Historical disdain for parties lingers in California's state election codes and permeates the conduct of elections, surfacing in initiatives that seek to empower individuals over organizations, such as Proposition 14 that recently reformed party primaries by opening them to all voters, regardless of their political party affiliation. It is also manifested in relatively weak party organizations, mounting numbers of independents, and in the candidate-centered nature of campaigning that requires extraordinary fund-raising muscle rather than robust assistance from a political party organization.

Parties are far from dormant, however, and the strident partisanship displayed in the legislature accentuates their viability. They are relevant at every level of government, from running elections to organizing government, and they still provide the most important voting cues for the average citizen. The ideological divisions they represent are real, and the fact that Democrats hold a distinct party registration advantage and swept statewide elections in 2010 signals their advantage over Republicans in the state. However, Democrats' electoral successes tend to mask citizens' growing detachment from parties. It remains to be seen whether the pairing of the open primary with a new redistricting process will result in campaigns, candidates, and winners who will exemplify the political moderation that characterizes most Californians.

Notes

1. E. E. Schattschneider, *Party Government: American Government in Action* (New York: 1942), 1.

2. "Voters" refers to a survey of those who participated in the November 2010 election. The statistic on trust in fellow voters comes from Mark Baldassare et al, "Californians and Their Government," December 2010, www.ppic.org/content/pubs/survey/S_1210MBS.pdf. For information about turnout by ethnic group, see: Public Policy Institute of California, "Just the Facts: California Voter and Party Profiles," September 2010, www.ppic.org/content/pubs/jtf/JTF_VoterProfilesJTF.pdf. For information about voters' perceptions about the initiative process, see Public Policy Institute of California, "Just the Facts: Californians and the Initiative Process," November 2008, www.ppic.org/content/pubs/jtf/JTF_InitiativeJTF.pdf.

3. Cross-filing, the practice of allowing candidates to file nomination papers with any party, appear on multiple ballots, and gain the nomination of more than one party was finally eliminated through legislative action in 1959, and a ban on pre-primary endorsements was found to be unconstitutional in 1989.

4. Mark Baldassare, "California's Post-Partisan Future," Public Policy Institute of California, January 2008, 2.

5. Data taken from the California Secretary of State, "Odd-numbered year report of registration, February 10, 2011," http://www.sos.ca.gov/elections/ror/ror-pages/ror-odd-year-11/hist-reg-stats.pdf.

6. Mark Baldassare et al., "Californians and Their Government." December 2010, Public Policy Institute of California, http://www.ppic.org/content/pubs/survey/S_1210MBS.pdf; and national election data compiled from National Election Pool poll results, reported on CNN Election Center 2008, www.cnn.com/ELECTION/2008/results/polls/#val=CAP00p1.

7. Mark Baldassare, "California's Post-Partisan Future," January 2008, Public Policy Institute of California, http://www.ppic.org/content/pubs/atissue/AI_108MBAI.pdf. Note that California party and voter profiles are compiled from eight statewide surveys conducted

between September 2009 and July 2010 and included 9,993 likely voters. See Public Policy Institute of California, "Just the Facts: California Voter and Party Profiles," September 2010, http://www.ppic.org/content/pubs/jtf/JTF_VoterProfilesJTF.pdf.

8. Baldassare, "California's Post-Partisan Future," 5.

9. The Public Policy Institute of California's party profiles are drawn from surveys conducted in 2008. See "Just the Facts: California's Partisan Divide." August 2008, www.ppic.org/content/pubs/jtf/JTF_CaDivideJTF.pdf.

10. National Conference of State Legislatures, "Redistricting Commissions: Legislative Plans," www.ncsl.org/?tabid=16617.

11. Data compiled from the California Secretary of State's Election Division.

12. Lou Cannon, *Ronnie and Jesse: A Political Odyssey* (New York: Doubleday, 1969), 99.

13. Based on 2008 and 2010 data, see www.followthemoney.org/database/state_overview.phtml?s=CA&y=2008 and www.followthemoney.org/database/StateGlance/state_candidates.phtml?s=CA&y=2010&f=0&so=a&p=6#sorttable. Averages reflect sums spent by winners. For the midterm 2010 election, the average was slightly lower for winning senate candidates, at approximately $885,000.

Political Engagement

Connecting Citizens to Politics

The Greek words *demos* and *kratos,* or democracy, translates literally as "the people rule." Democracy is therefore rightly associated with voting, but self-governance requires more than filling in bubbles on a ballot. Being informed, discussing public affairs, and contacting elected officials are essential elements of self-governance that allow a citizenry's will, demands, and needs to be expressed, and these are but a few ways a person might engage politically. Subgroups of citizens with similar interests try to influence the political system through into political parties (the subject of the chapter 9) or organized interest groups, of which there are thousands in the state of California alone. In addition, mass media play a critical role in linking residents, interest groups, and government through distributing and analyzing information that influences how Californians behave politically.

Sources of News

Californians know extremely little about state politics unless the subject is a crisis or an election, and their attitudes, opinions, and beliefs about government are molded by the way public affairs are reported and analyzed in the press. The most relevant media sources are several large **newspaper** operations (*Los Angeles Times, The Sacramento Bee,* and several other major city papers) that provide some in-depth treatment of issues; **minority newspapers** and publications, such as *La Opinion*; local **television** coverage that tends to be scant, sporadic, and celebrity- or event-driven, except on election night; **Internet sites and blogs** providing ongoing updates, news compendiums, and analyses; and **radio** programs (for example "The California Report" by KQED is aired during commute times on public radio, as is the conservative "John and Ken" talk show). Other sources such as Cal-Span, the state's version of C-Span that provides cable feeds of committee hearings and floor debates, attract tiny audiences. Until megastar Arnold Schwarzenegger assumed the governorship, all but a few news bureaus had closed their operations in the capitol.

National trends affect news coverage and consumption, with **media consolidation** topping the list. "One-newspaper cities" abound following the disappearance of local papers during the past few decades, and most of the state's big newspapers are owned by out-of-state corporations. Much of what's reported is delivered in bullet points and based on government reports and press releases, as well as the Associated Press (AP) wire service. The overall trend toward reporting news in entertaining ways, or "**infotainment**," has also entered the mix. At least 8 percent of registered California voters admit to getting their information about California politics from *The Daily Show* on Comedy Central.[1]

It is also worth noting that nontraditional forms of communication facilitate the flow of information between representatives and their constituents, and among the citizenry. Elected officials' **e-mail** updates and action alerts, **e-newsletters**, **tweets**, **texts**, and **links** to articles or videos let people know how to get involved, voice their opinions, or announce their whereabouts. They allow representatives to communicate efficiently with many constituents at once and deliver news quickly. Links embedded in e-mails provide recipients an easy way to sign petitions, donate, or send mail to their representatives. Social networking for political purposes is not without drawbacks, however. For instance, tweeted or texted information tends to be shallow and lacking context, misinformation can spread like wildfire without the ability to retract it fully, and public authorities tend to "script" their appearances because they know their gaffes could be broadcast on YouTube. It remains to be seen whether participation based on social networking will yield the same kinds of benefits associated with traditional forms of political participation, such as higher levels of political interest, feeling that one can make a difference, and closer ties and trust among community members.

Despite the proliferation of social networking and expanded forms of instant communication, like other Americans, most Californians by their own admission do not follow state politics closely. Fewer than half of registered voters (41 percent) say they follow what's going on in government and politics most of the time, and about a quarter do not follow politics at all.[2] Most people still get their information from television, including cable stations, but the Internet is overtaking television as the primary news source for younger adults (34 percent Internet, 29 percent television), and newspapers are struggling to maintain circulation as people increasingly read them online.[3] Interestingly, Republicans seem to pay more attention to politics than Democrats (see chart), Northern Californians are more politically attentive than Southern Californians, and those who identify with the Tea Party movement

TABLE 10.1 How Much California Voters Pay Attention to Government/Public Offices

	Percent paying attention		
	Most of the time	Some of the time	Hardly at all
All registered voters	41%	33%	25%
Party registration			
Democrat	41	34	24
Republican	50	29	20
Non-partisan/other	30	37	32
Tea Party identification			
Identify a lot*	77	18	5
Identify some	46	37	17
Don't identify	35	34	30
Area			
Southern California	35	37	27
Northern California	50	28	32
Gender			
Male	47	30	22
Female	36	36	27
Age			
18–29	15	39	45
30–39	30	41	28
40–49	41	31	27
50–64	49	33	17
65 or older	63	25	11
Race/ethnicity			
White, non-Hispanic	47	30	22
Latino	25	40	33
Education			
High School graduate or less	31	31	36
Some college/college graduate	41	36	23
Post-graduate work	50	30	20
Household income			
Less than $20,000	26	37	36
$20,000–$39,999	34	36	29
$40,000–59,999	40	36	24
$60,000 or more	48	32	21

* Small sample base.

Note: Figures have been rounded, and respondents with no opinion are not displayed in the table; percentages do not add to 100 percent.

Source: *The Field Poll,* completed June 3–13, 2011, using a random sample of 950 registered California voters; sampling error +/– 3.3 percentage points.

pay close attention to politics—more so than any other subgroup. Other news consumption patterns reflect behavior that has been well documented: older, white, more educated, and wealthier citizens pay closer attention to government affairs. These trends demonstrate that **political interest** makes a huge difference in helping people connect to politics; those who feel the impact of policies, recognize the immediate relevance of state government, and feel as if they can make a difference tend to seek more information that can lead to becoming involved politically.

Engagement, Disengagement, and Forms of Participation

Feeling informed contributes to the sense that one can personally make a difference by participating in public affairs and thus provides a stepping stone to active political participation. In addition to voting, which will be discussed below, Californians partake in a wide range of political activities. **Volunteering** for any number of community-oriented purposes or organizations, such as the Parent-Teacher Association (PTA), scouting, team sports, soup kitchens, hospital auxiliaries, or historical societies, for example, is a civic activity with political implications as it helps strengthen communities by building trust, networks, and mutual understanding. At the lowest level of political involvement, individuals might **discuss politics** with their friends and family, indicate their political **likes and dislikes** on their Facebook pages, try to **influence how others vote,** post a **yard sign,** or sport a campaign **sticker or tee** shirt. Higher up the scale, Californians **sign petitions** and may do so easily when electronic versions show up in their e-mail inboxes. It takes progressively larger investments to **call** or write **e-mails** or letters to elected officials in response to their solicitations for feedback or voluntarily to complain about a problem or ask for help with an issue; **attend local meetings; attend rallies,** demonstrations or speeches; **work with an informal group** to address a local problem; **work for a campaign;** or even **donate** to campaigns or incumbents. Only the most dedicated become **active party members or officers.**

The same kinds of socioeconomic factors associated with use of news media are also strongly related to general forms of political participation—patterns that are mirrored at the national level. In addition to the variables already mentioned, homeownership and length of residence are also positively associated with civic behavior and activism; retirees and older residents who have lived in the same house for more than two decades are among the most reliable, vocal political participants. Nationwide in 2008, about half (45 percent) of citizens said they had tried to influence how others voted; only 9 percent reported that they had attended a meeting, rally, or speech; and 4 percent had worked for a party or candidate.[4] In California under half (39 percent) said they had attended meetings, fewer said they had donated to campaigns and attended rallies, and the fewest (under 10 percent) said they had worked for a political party. Stark differences in the political behavior of major ethnic groups from surveys asking respondents to self-report their political activities, with whites edging out other groups in all but two categories: attending meetings and attending rallies.[5]

These differences also surface when looking at citizens' communication with state representatives. Although the number of phone calls, e-mails, faxes, and other contacts depends on factors such as how aggressively the representative solicits requests for help, issues the legislature is considering, the time of year (budget or holiday season for example), and the activity level of organized groups in a geographic region, it is clear that districts containing higher-income, more highly educated populations take time to ask for help with issues that concern them. For instance, "Senate District A" is represented by a senator who has an active outreach program, and the district includes a high concentration of white, very educated, higher-income residents. Recall that each senate district contains over 930,000 people. Per month, the senator receives approximately eleven hundred e-mails (many of which are "form letters" encouraged by organized groups), about fourteen hundred phone calls and handles approximately sixty cases, which are issues that must be dealt with by the office staff or a state worker, such as locating a lost disability income check. "Senate District B," on the other hand, is more ethnically diverse, is lower in income, contains many non-English speakers, has a less-educated population, and its senator is less aggressive about encouraging contacts from constituents. This senator receives very few e-mails and approximately one hundred calls per month, and about half of the contacts require casework by the office staff.[6] In any case, very few people take time to contact their representatives, and even fewer make "meaningful" inquiries that require the attention of either the staff or the representative.

Thus, rates of participation differ markedly by socioeconomic status: overall, those who are white, established, educated, and affluent speak louder than the

Students at the Butte Community College campus are shown organizing in support of education as the state's shrinking budget threatened to bring higher fees and fewer classes.

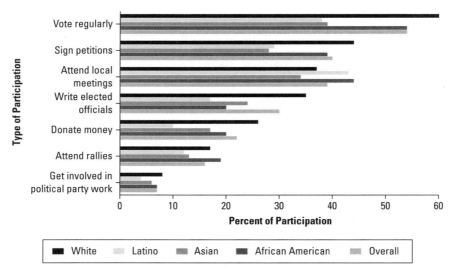

FIGURE 10.1

Political Participation by Race and Ethnicity

Sources: Public Policy Institute of California Statewide Surveys, August, October, November 2002.

rest. On the other hand, while disengaging from politics can certainly be a conscious choice, *not participating* is associated with these same factors, which are often beyond an individual's control. Poverty and lack of education can produce a reduced skill set, including language deficits, a smaller knowledge base, a lower sense of efficacy, fewer chances to be contacted or mobilized, and/or less disposable time to participate in activities. These disparities also surface among ethnic/racial groupings. Those who feel as if they will never be heard will hardly waste their time trying to voice their opinions, and continuing disengagement leads to even greater disparities in skills and resources apportioned to them, and high levels of frustration and political apathy.

Major Voting Trends

In representative democracy the act of voting provides a critical check on officeholders, as it not only offers a means to reject undesirable representatives but also supplies cues about what policies a constituency prefers. In a direct democracy the voters represent themselves and "check" each other through the act of voting, but the majority still wins. For these reasons, who votes in a hybrid democracy such as California's has profound implications for electoral outcomes, policymaking in the public interest, and, ultimately, the quality of government and representation.

The California electorate does not represent all Californians, nor does it reflect the population's size, growth, or diversity.[7] Not all residents are citizens, about

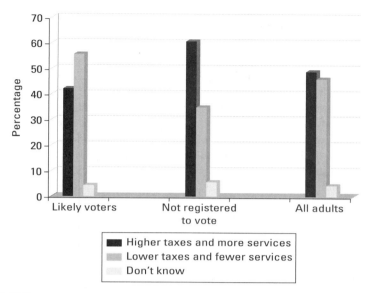

FIGURE 10.2

Differing Perceptions about the Role of Government

Source: Public Policy Institute of California, "Californias and their Government, Statewide Survey," January 2011.

25 percent of the eligible population doesn't register to vote, and not all eligible voters vote in every election. What's more, those who cast ballots generally hold very different views about the proper role of government than those who do not. For instance, when asked whether it was preferable to pay higher taxes and have a state government that provides more services, or pay lower taxes and have a state government that provides fewer services, a majority of voters preferred the smaller government option. However, a majority of infrequent voters preferred more services and higher taxes, as did a clear majority (60 percent) of those who were not registered to vote.

These ideological differences are magnified in low-turnout elections. Stand-alone municipal elections have distinctly low turnout rates that usually range between 20 and 35 percent, exceptions being higher regular turnout in some active communities and in the occasional "hot" local elections featuring a distinctive candidate, energizing issue, or scandal; measures perceived as mundane will yield even lower turnout. Presidential elections, super-charged ballot issues such as gay marriage, and high-profile events such as the 2003 recall lure many more voters than "off-year" midterm elections, special elections, or primaries, which draw more loyal partisans. Turnout rates also mask the phenomenon of "roll-off," or fewer votes being cast for more obscure offices listed nearer the end of a ballot.

Immigration has changed the state's demography far more quickly than it has contributed to changes in the voting population, and political observers are still waiting for the "sleeping giant" to awaken (the reference is to a potentially huge Latino voting bloc). For instance, although non-Hispanic whites total just over 40 percent of California's resident population, they comprise approximately two-thirds of all voters, who are in general also slightly older, native born, and more conservative than nonvoters. In contrast, nearly 40 percent of Californians are Latino, but fewer than 20 percent of voters are.[8] As with other forms of participation, differences in turnout are also related to **disposable time** (most people who don't vote work more than forty hours per week, and it takes time to become educated about the issues and candidates and to vote) and structural factors such as **registration requirements**, **timing of elections**, and the **perceived importance** of a given election. **Political interest** and **beliefs about government** are significant predictors of voting: two out of three nonvoters and infrequent voters believe that politics are controlled by special interests, and many of them (20 percent) find no candidates to believe in.[9] Having friends and family who value voting or **living in a "pro-voting" culture** also matters: two-thirds of those who speak Spanish and rarely vote also say that their friends hardly ever talk about politics. Other important variables are **age** (younger residents are more likely to be Latino and these groups vote at the lowest rates), **nativity** (native-born residents are more likely to vote than foreign-born citizens), **education**, **home ownership**, and **income**. Almost all of these characteristics

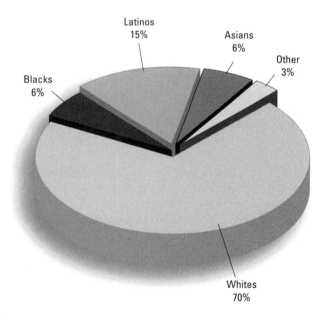

FIGURE 10.3

Ethnic Makeup of California's Likely Voters

Source: Public Policy Institute of California.

are at least indirectly related to immigrant status, and the "haves" out-shout the "have-nots" in elections.

It is also important to note that different combinations of voters produce different electoral outcomes. Voters grouped into assembly districts choose candidates who tend to reflect their characteristics and preferences, and, as a result, elected legislators resemble those localized voters. Initiative voters, on the other hand, hail from the entire state, and their votes reflect a different set of characteristics and preferences. The same is true for governors and statewide executives whose constituency is the entire state.

Interest Groups: Direct and Indirect Connections

Most citizens are unaware that they are indirectly linked to government through the interests they share with organized groups. Interest groups representing practically every aspect of the human experience advocate for government policies

TABLE 10.2 Top 15 Donors to All California Candidates by Industry, 2010

Industry	Total amount donated
Electric utilities	$50,741,914
Public sector unions	$45,668,817
General business	$29,601,840
General trade unions	$28,799,146
Insurance	$24,469,224
Pro-environment	$18,885,024
Oil & gas	$18,490,992
Securities & investments	$17,650,798
Lawyers & lobbyists	$14,219,630
Construction	$17,016,517
Education	$13,288,139
TV/movie production/distribution	$12,358,758
Real estate	$10,348,227
Computer equipment & services	$10,057,236
Health services & products/hospital/pharma	$10,865,951

Excludes transfers from parties, candidates, and self-financing.

Source: www.followthemoney.org; www.followthemoney.org/database/state_overview.phtml?s=CA&y=2008.

BOX 10.1 **The Power of Organized Interests**

The California Teachers Association: Major Player in Education

If education was in the news this morning, chances are the powerful California Teachers Association (CTA) had something to do with publicizing it. As the state's largest professional employee organization, representing some 325,000 teachers, school counselors, and librarians, the union helps bargain for higher salaries and benefits in local districts and provides assistance in contract disputes. As an advocacy group the CTA is committed to "enhance the quality of education for students" and "advance the cause of free, universal, and quality public education"* through influencing state education policy.

Closely aligned with Democratic interests, the CTA participates at all stages of the bill-passage process by writing bills, testifying before committees, shaping legislation through suggesting amendments, donating to initiative campaigns, mobilizing citizens to support measures, and encouraging legislators either to support or oppose bills. Most of this work is done through lobbyists, but members also are highly active, holding public demonstrations in local districts and loud rallies at the state capitol, organizing massive postcard campaigns, calling legislators to voice their views, and contributing through the union to state legislators' and initiative campaigns. In 2009 the union spent $6.9 million on Proposition 1A; the measure would have guaranteed school funding from a newly created special reserve fund. When the governor proposed altering

When teachers speak, Democratic legislators—and sometimes the governor—listen. As the state's largest union, the California Teachers Association (CTA) exerts tremendous influence over education policy and funding. When education funding was cut in 2009, the group spent millions airing television ads in protest. Further cuts prompted the CTA to organize statewide rallies and demonstrations in support of education in spring 2011.

Proposition 98 to balance the budget in summer 2009, the CTA roared to life with a statewide ad campaign attacking the governor's plan to "rob millions of dollars from public schools." During the busy mid-term election year of 2010, the CTA made large donations to local school bond initiative campaigns, the Democratic Party, and statewide initiatives that they supported—$14.3 million in all. The CTA also retained seven or so lobbyists costing about $1.5 million from 2009–2010.

*Sources: California Teachers Assocation, www.cta.org; California Secretary of State, http://www.sos.ca.gov/.

California Chamber of Commerce: Major Player in Business

Ever heard of a "job killer" bill? The California Chamber of Commerce has, and it does everything in its power to identify and kill *them* before they impose new "expensive and unnecessary" regulations on California businesses. What is the chamber, and why is it so powerful?

The state's largest and arguably most important business organization boasts a membership of almost fifteen thousand California-based companies, from local shops to the Disney Corporation, enterprises that employ a quarter of the state's private sector workforce. Boasting the motto of "helping California business do business," the chamber tries to help shape relevant laws or administrative rules by educating state and federal lawmakers about a law's impact on companies and the potential effects of bills or changes to current laws. It also donates to sympathetic candidates and office holders, supports ballot campaigns, and helps incumbents through sponsoring events, among other activities. Unlike many other professional associations, such as the CTA (which represents individuals), the chamber's members are companies that often pursue additional lobbying activities on measures that affect them. The chamber reported payments to an average of seven in-house lobbyists from 2009–2010 as totaling $1.05 million and lobbying expenditures for the first half of 2011 as $683,000, though this figure represents a fraction of what businesses spend to protect their interests in California. For example, the Disney pays close to $500,000 a year for ongoing lobbying activities.

Sources: California Chamber of Commerce, www.calchamber.com; California Secretary of State, http://www.sos.ca.gov/.

Bringing attention to business-related issues is part of CalChamber's strategy to influence the lawmaking and regulatory environment. President and CEO, Allan Zaremberg, promotes this objective through press interviews.

that will advance or protect their causes, and the benefits or changes they seek often extend to anyone who shares a key characteristic. For example, a typical California college student is "represented" in the public sphere by a plethora of unobserved but well-organized "special" interests, among them the university or college itself; the city, county, and region in which the student resides; hobby-, sports-, or activity-related groups such as the National Collegiate Athletic Association; groups based on demographic characteristics such as economic status, ethnicity, employment, religion, and more; consumer- or business-oriented organizations relating to financial habits or earnings; health-related groups concerned with conditions such as diabetes or allergies; values-based associations focusing on rights, the environment, moral issues; and too many more to name. Stronger links are forged through actual membership in a union or association for working adults or professionals, such as the mighty California Correctional Peace Officers Association (CCPOA), which represents thirty thousand prison guards and parole officers, or the 160,000-member California Association of Realtors, which facilitates state licensing requirements and pushes for or resists changes in laws and tax policies that will affect realtors or their clients. Many other powerful special interests are individual corporations and umbrella associations for businesses, such as the California Farm Bureau or the California Medical Association.

Special interests are not all equal, however, and some in California carry disproportionate political weight because of advantages based on their resources, size, and/or perceived importance. Among the most active "special interests" in Sacramento are **government entities** that carry out state programs for thousands or millions of Californians. Public officials or specialists working for cities, counties, and special districts communicate their concerns to legislators directly through lawmakers' staff or by testifying about bills in committee hearings. As public authorities, their voices are valued in wider public debates over policy. **Money,** or the ability to donate to candidates individually or through political action committees (PACs) or fund independent campaigns through television ads and mailers, helps groups establish their reputation and gain access to legislators and administrators. Money also allows groups to hire **professional lobbyists** who can "educate" legislators and their staff about the negative or positive effects pending legislation may have on their clients, research and draft client-friendly legislation for lawmakers to sponsor, be persuasive witnesses in committee hearings where bills are vetted, and buy expensive tickets to legislators' fundraisers (lobbyists may not directly donate to candidates). Large membership groups such as unions bring the power of many **potential voters** to bear in their negotiations with government officials, as representatives prefer to please large, politically active constituencies.

Any group or business that has the **ability to mobilize voters and influence public opinion** also possesses great advantages. Large-scale influence can be exerted through **public relations** efforts involving mailers, ads, e-mail blasts, letter-writing campaigns, rallies, special events, or even sponsorship of charitable events or community facilities (where corporate logos can be prominently displayed). Other special interests have privileged status because of the significant economic activity they generate—such as large corporations, unions, energy companies, and Native American casinos—or by their large employee base (defense manufacturers, large retail chains). These well-heeled few skew the playing field in their favor. In state politics as elsewhere, organization, money, and status amplify voices and provide critical linkages to decision makers. Along with resource-poor groups, the unorganized are the biggest losers in politics.

Conclusion: An Evolving Political Community

In addition to political parties, mass media, e-mail, Internet sites, social networking applications, and even interest groups create the means for citizens to connect to government affairs, officials, and each other. Established news corporations still have the furthest reach among Californians through television, newspapers, and radio, but very few people pay rapt attention to state politics, many pay no attention at all, and those in between are scarcely listening or do so only when crises, scandals, or elections occur. Being informed helps empower citizens to be politically active, and there is plenty of room for more citizen participation at all levels of government, because even though political scientists disagree about the minimum levels of knowledge, trust, or engagement needed to sustain a governing system for the long term, they generally recognize that "inputs" taking the form of civic involvement and political participation generally lead to more positive government "outputs." As it stands, rich corporations, well-heeled unions, and large, organized, resource-rich groups are perpetual, outsized contributors to California's political system and, consequently, benefit from their inputs. As the saying goes, the squeaky wheel gets the oil.

The most recognizable form of participation—voting—carries intrinsic value as a democratic exercise and plays a vital role in linking citizens to their representatives. Election results provide winners with clear indications of a constituency's political leanings. Uneven levels of participation, however, and higher rates of nonvoting among Latinos contribute to the governing dilemmas of policymakers as they weigh their responsibilities to serve the greater public interest but also respond to those who actually cast their ballots and are politically active. Until the electorate more accurately reflects the entirety of the state's population, elected officials' decisions will continue to reflect the political, cultural, geographic, and demographic biases of those who vote. Expanding the electorate and raising levels of political participation are sure-fire ways California's government might be made more accountable and representative in the search for greater governability.

Notes

1. Mark DiCamillo and Mervin Field, *The Field Poll*, "Release #2382, Monday, June 27, 2011." Survey was conducted on 950 registered voters in California by telephone in English and Spanish, June 3–13, 2011, sampling error +/– 3.3%.

2. *The Field Poll*, June 27, 2011.

3. Public Policy Institute of California, "Californians' News and Information Sources, PPIC Statewide Survey," October 2010. Survey included 2,002 adults (margin of error +/– 3.1%).

4. Source: The American National Election Study, "Guide to Public Opinion and Electoral Behavior, 1956–2008," www.electionstudies.org/nesguide/toptable/tab6b_4.htm.

5. The most recent statewide survey regarding Californians and their political behavior was conducted in 2002 by the Public Policy Institute of California, reported in S. Ramakrishnan and Mark Baldassare, "The Ties that Bind: Changing Demographics and Civic Engagement in California," 2004, http://www.ppic.org/content/pubs/report/R_404KRR.pdf. With the advent of e-mail and social networking, it is likely that political activities that can easily be conducted through these media, such as signing petitions or donating to campaigns, have increased substantially since this survey was conducted.

6. This snapshot of constituent contacts was provided by a senate chief of staff who fielded inquiries from several other chiefs of staff in August 2011, and it is not meant to be a scientific survey of all offices. Rather, the data provide an impression of the variance among offices in terms of activity level and are approximations. Averages are difficult to verify because "no day is the same," and tracking these contacts rigorously would require significant investments of time and efforts by office staff.

7. Mark Baldassare, *California's Exclusive Electorate* (San Francisco: Public Policy Institute of California, 2006).

8. Public Policy Institute of California, "Just the Facts: Latino Voters in California," August 2008, 1. In 2008, when turnout reached its highest point since 1972, the *Los Angeles Times* reported that actual turnout among Latinos was 18 percent, whereas among whites it was 63 percent. See www.latimes.com/news/politics/la-110608-me-superchart-g,0,7151660.graphic (data from National Election Pool). More recent polls (USC/*Los Angeles Times*, November 2010) peg 2008 Latino turnout at closer to 16 percent. Totals are based on exit polls that rely on self-reported voting history and self-identified ethnic background. Differences in self-reporting have led to notable conflicts among polling results (see *The Field Poll* and USC/*Los Angeles Times* exit polls).

9. Reported statistics on nonvoters and infrequent voters in this section come from the California Voter Foundation, "California Voter Participation Survey," 2005, http://www.calvoter.org/issues/votereng/votpart/index.html.

CHAPTER 11

Concluding Thoughts: Political Paradoxes and Governability

I s California ungovernable? Is California too big *not* to fail? Governability suggests a good fit between the demands of a state's people and what its institutions deliver, that representatives understand their constituents' needs, and that decision makers grasp the dimensions of pressing problems and devise fair, responsible, timely solutions. Governability is enabled by rules that encourage participation, deliberation, and compromise, or by some combination of strong leadership and cooperation. California falls far short on each count.

Though reports of the Golden State's death have been exaggerated (to borrow a phrase from Mark Twain), predictions of its demise continue to swirl amid clear signs of its government's failings, and it has come dangerously close to the precipice of economic ruin more than once. Extremely low trust in government, partisan standoffs, yearly multibillion-dollar structural budget deficits that dwarf the economies of small countries, a gross backlog of unfulfilled infrastructure needs, and growing bond debt contribute to the perception that California's government is not working and that without full-scale overhaul little will change. Voter exasperation surfaces regularly in polls showing extremely low approval ratings for state institutions and in initiatives that hammer politicians.

Continuing economic woes merely compound what is at best an impractical political situation. Having embraced the power of direct democracy, slices of California—that is, some percentage of eligible voters rather than all adult residents—make decisions for the entire state as a parallel lawmaking institution, one far less deliberative than its counterpart in Sacramento. In fact, what was supposed to be a stopgap measure for keeping legislators in check is now an overworked policymaking machine, the gears of which are oiled by campaign donations and shifted by an electorate not fully representative of the state's diverse population. In a system dominated by special interests parading as public interests, meeting the state's actual needs becomes more difficult.

Direct democracy and representative democracy live in a state of uneasy tension, and imbalances in the distribution of power between voters and policymakers are inevitable. This can be seen most clearly in voter-imposed rules that restrict legislators' budgeting power, such as guaranteed funding for big-ticket items like schools, but also in practically unattainable thresholds for raising tax revenues (two-thirds voter approval for initiative tax measures and two-thirds of the legislature for revenue-raising bills). Incremental ballot-box changes stymie comprehensive approaches to governing. California's hybrid democracy is an institutional paradox, a seemingly illogical development that calls the state's governability into question. So is the notion that Californians demand strong and efficient leadership from all elected officeholders, yet they choose to limit authorities' power and therefore the ability of these officials to perform efficiently and effectively. Ironically, the layering of rules makes the strong leadership that voters desire even more remote.

California politics is riddled with other paradoxes that go a long way toward explaining the current state of affairs. For example, Californians generally distrust politicians and are averse to political conflict, so they continue to reach for ways to take politicians—and politics, for that matter—"out" of politics; they resort to passing initiatives like term limits and open primaries that will automatically remove people from office at prescribed intervals and lessen party control. Disappointment and resentment in the body politic continue to grow, however, because political systems are by nature designed to expose conflicting interests in the struggle to reach consensus, and the people not only need politicians to govern what is effectively one of the largest countries in the world, they need to organize in order to win, and parties provide that reliable structure. Nevertheless, younger Californians are unconvinced that parties matter, and increasingly they are registering as "decline-to-state" voters.

Historically speaking, Californians' choices also reflect unrealistic expectations about the capabilities of governing institutions. On the whole, for instance, Californians presume that rooting out government waste will offset necessary revenues for government services, as if saving millions of dollars could compensate for not raising billions.

Furthermore, having heard for years the abstract complaint about state insolvency, and having mostly been spared deep budget cuts or steep tax increases to align state spending with shrinking revenues, many Californians have remained unprepared for real fiscal austerity. Citizens bear the pain in the form of shortened school years, lower pensions, loss of health coverage, long-delayed court dates, or higher fees at state parks, but often the complexity of funding the state through taxes, tax incentives, credits, cuts, transfers, grants, and borrowing do not make budget cuts more acceptable or understandable when they finally hit home.

Paradoxically, Californians also expect that the public good will be served when their personal needs are met. This may be possible with a government service like public education, a "good" that yields private gains with long-term public benefits, but it does not produce sustainable economic policies. To wit, Californians prefer to pay lower sales, income, and property taxes in the short term, creating chronic underfunding of local and state governments that are burdened with meeting basic sanitation, education, health, transportation, and safety needs. Moreover, this tendency has resulted in a shift away from policies that impose upfront costs and toward long-term bond debt that costs twice as much in the long run, generating interest payments that place stress on the state's general fund by siphoning off money that could be used for other necessary budget items.

Quite apart from the institutional aspects of governing are socioeconomic and political issues that determine the state's political state of affairs—issues that involve more than thirty-eight million people who place myriad, conflicting, and ever-changing demands on the state. The multiethnic mix of children signals momentous change in the near future: nonwhites have accounted for all the growth in the youth population in the last ten years. It is estimated that California will be an absolute majority Latino state in the next decade, and the population will approach fifty million people by 2025.[1] How will decision makers nurture the educated workforce that will be needed to drive the state's service-based economy? Will voters be willing to extend helping hands to those on the bottom end of the socioeconomic scale? At least one in seven Californians will be sixty-five years of age or older by that time: How will the state provide for a large elderly population that places immense demands on health care systems? Already the state administration has estimated that to accommodate such growth, approximately $500 billion will be required to rebuild and expand aging transportation, school, water, and other systems in the next twenty years. How will Californians be able to raise that kind of cash?[2]

In many ways, political reforms brought California to this point, and political reforms will help transform the future. Yet institutional reforms can only go so far. Rules set boundaries for decision making but do not determine the choices people make, and choices must be based on realistic understanding about government's capabilities if the state's policies and laws are to work. Voters' expectations and attitudes about government underscore California's ungovernability.

Overall, California government faces the same challenges as other states. What makes it distinct are the scope and scale of its issues, a hybrid governing structure in which voters can change the rules of the game for representatives, and constraints placed on authorities' power that range from term limits to supermajority thresholds that sacrifice majority will to the rival demands of a minority (usually the minority party) and suppress strong leadership. The issues are mostly the same across the nation, however, and they pose enormous challenges for state government now and for the foreseeable future. The extent to which these policy questions overwhelm competent elected officials is a measure of California's ungovernability:

- Education: Only an educated workforce can sustain a sophisticated, diverse, service-oriented, modern economy. California continues to spend less on its K–12 students than almost all other states, and hard economic times mean fewer days of instruction, lower pay for teachers, lack of instructional or supplementary materials, and shortages of reliable afterschool care and programs. How will the state prepare its students to meet the state's and nation's changing economic needs? The fastest-growing segment of the population is Latino, but as a group these students lag behind in graduation rates and test scores. How will achievement gaps be closed? How will graduation rates be improved? Deep budget cuts also threaten to destabilize the state's premier college and university systems by carving away essential funding, much of which is used to hire and support the "best and brightest" who do research, teach, and prepare students for the workforce. State education is still a bargain compared to other states, but California's master plan for providing tuition-free higher education has been abandoned. How will the state's college and university system compare nationally after budgets are slashed? How will students' education be affected in the short and long terms?
- Immigration: California's immigrant population is the largest in the nation, with one in four current residents having been born outside the United States. Will voters be willing to extend the same public benefits to immigrant groups that many of them enjoy, and if not, how might a service economy accommodate massive numbers of low-skilled, unemployed, low-educated groups that would require state services to fulfill basic needs, from food to housing to employment?
- Environment: Climate change threatens California's basic lifelines. Erratic weather patterns are difficult to plan for. Rising temperatures bring less rain and lighter snowpack, as well as limited water supplies for thirsty farms, manufacturing plants, and homes. Alternatively, a late, heavy snowpack can produce severe (and costly) flooding. Volatile weather patterns place stress on traditional recreation and tourism and related industries. Lower rainfall increases the risk of wildfires in bone-dry areas and increases airborne fine particle pollution; wildlife unaccustomed to higher than average temperatures cannot quickly adjust, so biodiversity suffers. Rising sea levels threaten a densely populated coastline and imperil the delta agricultural region (the source of drinking water for two-thirds of Californians and irrigation for 750,000 acres of croplands) with rising levels of salinity. California adopted a stringent law that takes a first stab at addressing greenhouse gases (AB 32), and although it survived a ballot-box challenge, it remains under siege by those who object to regulations that will likely increase certain business costs. Will California lawmakers withstand these contests and go far enough

to curb the human-made greenhouse gas emissions directly contributing to these environmental changes, and will other states follow? Can California make necessary investments to bring about a "green" economy without creating a hostile business environment? Can the government adequately respond and the economy readjust when environmental crises like earthquakes, heat waves, extensive wildfires, extended droughts, and torrential rains and resulting mudslides hit in quick succession?

- Water: Between droughts and floods, policymakers have a hard time managing storage and distribution systems that move water from north to south, dealing with water scarcity that pits urban against agricultural users, and addressing contamination from chemicals in farmland runoff and urban activity. Neighboring states and Mexico have prolonged disputes over equitable distribution of the Colorado River and estuaries. Degraded wetlands are the norm, as are declining native fish populations and inexplicable fish die-offs that are increasing in number. In many parts of the Sacramento-San Joaquin delta region, where millions of people and animals reside and fertile lands are farmed, catastrophic levee failure due to earthquakes or flooding is a palpable risk. How will extremely costly solutions be implemented? Will California's leaders at state and local levels be able to craft strategic plans that comprehensively address the entire state's long-term needs?

- Transportation: The nation's highest number of cars on roads and freeways travel California's roadways, which are the most congested in the United States. The Legislative Analyst's Office notes that many of California's 50,500 miles of roads have either reached or will soon reach the end of their useful life, and while CalTrans estimates the costs of needed repairs at $7.4 billion annually, a paltry $1.5 billion is allocated for repairs each year. Combined with trucks, buses, and farm and construction equipment, California's motorized vehicles also create dirty air that causes major respiratory illnesses. Despite major investments in public transit since the 1990s, there has been virtually no reduction in the number of miles travelled by residents, and only 5 percent of Californians use public transit. California's airports, seaports, and railway systems contribute to pollution levels as well, an inevitable consequence of having the nation's busiest port (Long Beach) that is a gateway to Asia and South America. Can lawmakers improve California's air and travel systems by making them cleaner, safer, more navigable, and more efficient, and can they do so in cost-effective ways? Can they ensure the safety of residents as those systems take on larger proportions? How long will it take to reduce the state's extreme backlog of needs, and at what cost?

Less than a generation ago, California government was held up as a distinguished model of efficiency and planning. The state's fairly quick reversal of fortunes is a testament to the power of rapidly changing social, economic, and political circumstances; the cumulative force of historical decisions; the power of culture; the consequences of rules; and the importance of collective choices. These conditions will continue to be at the heart of the policymaking that will define California's future and its governability.

Notes

1. Ellen Hanak and Mark Baldassare, *California 2025: Taking on the Future* (San Francisco: Public Policy Institute of California, 2005), 28.

2. Ellen Hanak. "Paying for Infrastructure." (San Francisco: Public Policy Institute of California, 2009), 1.

List of Counties, Including Population and Median Income per County*

County	Population	Median household income
Alameda	1,510,271	$68,258
Alpine	1,175	$45,391
Amador	38,091	$54,461
Butte	220,000	$41,196
Calaveras	45,578	$51,564
Colusa	21,419	$47,472
Contra Costa	1,049,025	$75,084
Del Norte	28,610	$38,252
El Dorado	181,058	$68,778
Fresno	930,450	$45,219
Glenn	28,122	$41,904
Humboldt	134,623	$35,985
Imperial	174,528	$37,846
Inyo	18,546	$44,090
Kern	839,631	$46,938
Kings	152,982	$44,102
Lake	64,665	$36,895
Lassen	34,895	$46,377
Los Angeles	9,818,605	$54,375
Madera	150,865	$42,769
Marin	252,409	$86,658
Mariposa	18,251	$42,775
Mendocino	87,841	$41,488
Merced	255,793	$39,922
Modoc	9,686	$34,290
Mono	14,202	$53,973
Monterey	415,057	$57,647
Napa	136,484	$66,970
Nevada	98,764	$57,250

County	Population	Median household income
Orange	3,010,232	*$71,735*
Placer	348,432	*$70,751*
Plumas	20,007	*$42,684*
Riverside	2,189,641	*$55,151*
Sacramento	1,418,788	*$52,502*
San Benito	55,269	*$61,281*
San Bernardino	2,035,210	*$52,137*
San Diego	3,095,313	*$60,103*
San Francisco	805,235	*$70,247*
San Joaquin	685,306	*$52,201*
San Luis Obispo	269,637	*$55,638*
San Mateo	718,451	*$84,678*
Santa Barbara	423,895	*$58,555*
Santa Clara	1,781,642	*$84,990*
Santa Cruz	262,382	*$60,816*
Shasta	177,223	*$42,552*
Sierra	3,240	*$41,788*
Siskiyou	44,900	*$39,218*
Solano	413,344	*$65,079*
Sonoma	483,878	*$61,985*
Stanislaus	514,453	*$48,550*
Sutter	94,737	*$48,073*
Tehama	63,463	*$38,179*
Trinity	13,786	*$33,546*
Tulare	442,179	*$39,876*
Tuolumne	55,365	*$48,027*
Ventura	823,318	*$71,246*
Yolo	200,849	*$56,120*
Yuba	72,155	*$40,947*

Sources: Population figures: U.S. Census Bureau, "State and County QuickFacts," 2010, http://quickfacts.census.gov/qfd/states/06000.html. Median income was reported in 2009. Figures in this table may differ from current Department of Finance estimates cited elsewhere in this book.

Current Constitutional Officers and Leaders of the Legislature, Including Salaries and Term Limits, October 2011

Constitutional Officers

Office	Officeholder	Term limit	Salary
Governor	Edmund "Jerry" G. Brown Jr. (D)	2018	$173,987
Lieutenant Governor	Gavin Newsom (D)	2018	$130,490
Secretary of State	Debra Bowen (D)	2014	$130,490
Attorney General	Kamala Harris (D)	2018	$151,127
Treasurer	Bill Lockyer (D)	2014	$139,189
Controller	John Chiang (D)	2014	$139,189
Insurance Commissioner	Dave Jones (D)		$139,189
Superintendent of Public Instruction	Tom Torlakson (D)	2018	$151,127
Members, Board of Equalization	Betty Yee (D); George Runner (R); Michelle Steel (R); Jerome Horton (D)	2014; 2018; 2014; 2018	$130,490

Leaders of the Legislature

Senate position	Officeholder	Term limit	Salary*
President pro Tempore	Darrell Steinberg (D)	2014	$109,584
Majority Leader	Ellen Corbett (D)	2014	$102,437
Minority Leader	Robert Dutton (R)	2012	$109,584

Leaders of the Legislature

Assembly position	Officeholder	Term limit	Salary*
Speaker	John Pérez (D)	2014	$109,584
Speaker pro Tempore	Fiona Ma (D)	2012	$95,291**
Minority Floor Leader	Connie Conway (R)	2014	$109,584

Sources: State of California and California Citizens Compensation Commission.

Note: Effective December 9, 2009, salaries for all statewide officials declined by 18 percent. The starred salaries listed above reflect this reduction.

* All legislators are entitled to receive a per diem payment of $142 for each day they work while their house is in session. Per diem amounts are set by the Victim Compensation and Government Claims Board and are intended to cover daily expenses associated with working away from home. Total amounts vary annually with the number of days in session, and by chamber. In 2009–2010 senators could earn up to $29,507 annually, and assembly members averaged $26,520 during the same period (four legislators do not accept per diem payments).

Source: Senate Rules Committee; Assembly Rules Committee.

**The Assistant Speaker, or Speaker pro Tempore, does not receive enhanced pay. All legislators who do not hold leadership positions earn $95,291 plus per diem.

Recent Governors, Senate Presidents pro Tempore, and Speakers of the Assembly

Governors of California, 1943–Present

Name	Party	Year(s)
Earl Warren	R	1943–1953
Goodwin J. Knight	R	1953–1959
Edmund G. Brown	D	1959–1967
Ronald Reagan	R	1967–1975
Edmund "Jerry" G. Brown Jr.	D	1975–1983
George Deukmejian	R	1983–1991
Pete Wilson	R	1991–1999
Gray Davis	D	1999–2003
Arnold Schwarzenegger	R	2003–2011
Edmund "Jerry" G. Brown Jr.	D	2011–

Presidents pro Tempore of the Senate, 1939–Present

Name	Party	Year(s)
Jerrold L. Seawell	R	1939–1947
Harold J. Powers	R	1947–1954
Clarence C. Ward	R	1954–1955
Ben Hulse	R	1955–1957
Hugh M. Burns	D	1957–1969
Howard Way	R	1969–1970
Jack Schrade	R	1970–1971
James R. Mills	D	1971–1981
David A. Roberti	D	1981–1994
Bill Lockyer	D	1994–1998
John L. Burton	D	1998–2004
Don Perata	D	2004–2009
Darrell Steinberg	D	2009–

Speakers of the Assembly, 1943–Present

Name	Party	Year(s)
Charles W. Lyon	R	1943–1946
Sam L. Collins	R	1947–1952
James W. Silliman	R	1953–1954
Luther H. Lincoln	R	1955–1958
Ralph M. Brown	D	1959–1961
Jesse M. Unruh	D	1961–1969
Robert T. Monagan	R	1969–1970
Bob Moretti	D	1971–1974
Leo T. McCarthy	D	1974–1980
Willie Brown	D	1980–1995
Doris Allen	R	1995
Brian Setencich	R	1995–1996
Curt Pringle	R	1996
Cruz M. Bustamante	D	1996–1998
Antonio Villaraigosa	D	1998–2000
Robert M. Hertzberg	D	2000–2002
Herb J. Wesson Jr.	D	2002–2004
Fabian Núñez	D	2004–2008
Karen Bass	D	2008–2010
John A. Pérez	D	2010–